THE SIGN
OF HIS COMING

Understanding the Olivet Discourse

Renald E. Showers

The Friends of Israel Gospel Ministry, Inc.

Library of Congress Catalog Card Number: 2016949881

ISBN: 978-0-915540-76-1

Second Printing.. 2017

Cover by Catie Perseo

Visit our website at www.foi.org.

TABLE OF CONTENTS

PREFACE

The Olivet Discourse that Christ delivered to several of His apostles at their request is a gold mine of information concerning what will happen on Earth through the end of this planet's history. When studied alongside other sections of Scripture, it answers 12 important questions:

1. What question did Jesus' disciples ask that prompted Jesus to deliver His Olivet Discourse?
2. Since the Bible presents two different gospels, which one must be preached before the Rapture?
3. What is the unparalleled time of trouble for the people of Israel?
4. What will cause the Antichrist's radical change from being Israel's protector to being its chief enemy?
5. What is Israel's role in the restoration of God's theocratic Kingdom to the world?
6. What will be God's purposes for bringing the nations of the world against Israel?
7. What is involved in the Day of the Lord concept?
8. How did some holy angels become evil?
9. What did the statement that Jesus was "like the Son of Man" imply concerning Him?
10. Who is the only person who knows the day and hour of Jesus' Second Coming?
11. What will happen to unsaved people on Earth when Jesus returns at His Second Coming?
12. What is the major thing Christ will do at His Second Coming after He rids the earth of Satan and all the fallen angels?

The purpose of this book is to present an accurate explanation of what Christ told His apostles regarding the future, which, consequently, helps us understand why the world is moving in the direction that it is today. I pray it will be a blessing to you.

Renald E. Showers

DIFFERENCES BETWEEN THE RAPTURE AND THE SECOND COMING

The Rapture of the Church	The Second Coming of Jesus
It is not mentioned in the Old Testament, only in the New.	It is mentioned in both Testaments (Jude 14).
It is a mystery (1 Cor. 15:51).	It is not a mystery.
It is pretribulational (occurs prior to the Tribulation).	It is posttribulational (occurs after the Tribulation, Rev. 19:11–16).
No prophecies or signs must be fulfilled prior to the event (1 Cor. 15:50–53; 1 Th. 4:16).	Many signs must be fulfilled prior to the event (Mt. 24:29–31; Rev. 6—19).
It is imminent (1 Cor. 1:7; Jas. 5:8).	It is not imminent; it takes place after the seven-year Tribulation (Mt. 24:29–31).
The archangel heralds the event (1 Th. 4:16).	Multitudes of angels return with Christ (Mt. 25:31).
Christ does not come to Earth; He comes "in the air" (1 Th. 4:16–17).	Christ returns to Earth (Zech. 14:4; Mt. 25:31).
Christ's appearance is not visible to people on Earth (1 Cor. 15:52; 1 Th. 4:16–17).	His appearance is dramatically visible to the entire world (Mt. 24:30; Rev. 1:7).
Christ comes for His church (Jn. 14:1–2; 1 Th. 4:16–17).	Christ comes with His church (Rev. 19:14).
Christ takes believers to heaven (Jn. 14:2–3; 1 Th. 4:17).	Believers remain on Earth to enter the Messianic Kingdom with Christ (Mt. 25:34).
The Rapture removes believers from Earth.	The Second Coming removes unbelievers from Earth.
Christians receive a glorified body, preparing them for eternity (1 Cor. 15:50–53).	All survivors of the Tribulation remain in their natural bodies (Isa. 65:20; Mt. 25:31–34).
It is a message of comfort and hope (1 Th. 4:18; Ti. 2:13).	It is a message of judgment (Rev. 19:11).
No divine judgments affect the earth.	Severe judgments afflict the earth (Rev. 6—19).
Believers are evaluated, rewarded, and married to Christ following the Rapture (1 Cor. 3:11–15; Rev. 19:7–9).	The nations are judged following the Tribulation (Ezek. 20:34; Mt. 25:32).
There is no mention of Satan in connection with the Rapture.	Satan is bound and cast into the bottomless pit for 1,000 years (Rev. 20:1–3).
The Tribulation begins after the Rapture, when the Antichrist makes a covenant with the nation of Israel (Dan. 9:27).	The Millennial Kingdom begins after Christ's Second Coming (Lk. 1:32–33).

This chart shows basic differences between the Rapture of the church and Christ's Second Coming, based on Scripture. It is by no means comprehensive.

CHAPTER 1

A Significant Question and Response

Matthew 24:1–8

A friend of mine once told me that, when she was a young college student who did not know the Lord, she used to go to a palm reader. She and her friends would pile into a car and drive an hour into the country to pay $10 a piece to a white-haired lady who lived on a farm and claimed she could see into their futures by reading the palms of their hands. That was in the 1960s.

Unfortunately, she probably would not have to drive that far today. It seems that too many American towns have at least one building in front of which hangs a shingle that claims a fortuneteller of some sort resides within and is open for business.

God, of course, condemns such "soothsayers" and those who use them (Dt. 18:10, 14; Isa. 2:6). Yet people seem to want to know the future. They want to know what lies ahead for them personally and for the world collectively. That is why books by the 16th-century, self-proclaimed French "seer," Nostradamus, are still in print; why people still write prodigiously about him; and why he was featured on the cover of *Time* magazine in 1999.

So what does lie ahead? What will the world be like years from now? Can anyone really know? And do we need to know?

Evidently, we do need to know because God Himself, the only One who knows, has revealed it in His Word; and contrary to the prognostications of so-called palm readers and soothsayers, His Word is truth (Ps. 119:160; Jn. 17:17). It can be trusted 100 percent of the time.

In His Word we can look into the future through the lens of an extremely significant discourse delivered by Jesus Christ to His disciples. The message is recorded in the Gospel of Matthew, chapters 24—25. Because Jesus spoke it "as He sat on the Mount of Olives" (24:3), it traditionally has been called the Olivet Discourse; and it unveils God's political and spiritual trajectories for the world.

Jesus delivered the discourse to His disciples, who wanted to know, "What will be the sign of Your coming, and of the end of the age?" (v. 3). It is a curious question because Jesus was with them. They must have understood He would be leaving them and that He would return. They also must have believed He had true knowledge of the future, or they would not have asked Him to tell them about the "end of the age."

The disciples, of course, were Jewish. They were steeped in Jewish history and culture, and though pagan Rome occupied the land God had promised them as an "everlasting possession" (Gen. 17:8; 48:4), their question revealed they still believed in the Jewish teaching that the "age" would end at the future coming of their Messiah—whom they rightly considered to be Jesus.

To answer their question, Jesus launched into an extensive description of the future Tribulation. He told them what lies ahead—what chaos and turmoil the world and the Jewish people in particular can expect—immediately before He returns to establish His Messianic Kingdom.

Some of what He told them parallels ancient rabbinical teaching. Much of it parallels many portions of both the Hebrew Scriptures and New Testament, showing clearly the cohesiveness and eternality of God's Holy Word.

Jesus also spoke of the "gospel of the kingdom" (Mt. 24:14), a concept that is sorely misunderstood today. Many people fail to understand there are two distinct gospels in Scripture: the gospel of 1 Corinthians 15 and the gospel of the Kingdom, the latter of which says nothing about Christ's death and resurrection. Its content is "Repent, because the kingdom of God is at hand." The Olivet Discourse declares, "This gospel of the kingdom will be preached in all the world . . ., and then the end will come" (Mt. 24:14).

The Tribulation—a seven-year period when God unleashes His wrath on unbelieving, unrepentant humanity—will purify the earth and produce a people fit to enter the thousand-year, Messianic, Davidic

Kingdom. It also, for the most part, will wrap up the cosmic battle Satan has been waging against God since time began.

All these elements play prominent roles in the Olivet Discourse, making it one of the most important sections of New Testament Scripture.

THE SETTING

In 18 BC Herod the Great, who ruled Judea for the Roman Empire, began a great project to rebuild the second Jewish Temple and enlarge the Temple complex in Jerusalem.[1] The project was so massive, in fact, that it was in its 46th year of construction during the first Passover of Jesus' ministry (Jn. 2:11–20). It was not completed until AD 64, six decades after Herod died in 4 BC.[2]

The final Temple area consisted of approximately 26 acres of land.[3] An historian indicated that the Jewish people "were proud of the great shrine," with "its splendor," and that Herod's Temple "ranked among the marvels of the Augustan world."[4] A rabbi wrote, "One who did not see Herod's Temple missed seeing the most beautiful building in the world."[5]

One day, after Jesus left the Temple, His disciples approached Him to point out "the various buildings in the temple area" (Mt. 24:1). As Jews, they no doubt were proud of the complex. As they were observing the buildings, Jesus said to them, "Do you not see all these things? Assuredly, I say to you, not one stone shall be left here upon another, that shall not be thrown down" (v. 2). His statement must have stunned them. They probably were thinking, *How can He make such an ominous declaration, in light of the fact that the Temple project isn't even completed yet?*

Three years later, on the day of Jesus' triumphal entry into Jerusalem, days before His crucifixion, He made a parallel and prophetic statement when He saw the city and wept over it:

> *If you had known, even you, especially in this your day, the things that make for your peace! But now they are hidden from your eyes. For days will come upon you when your enemies will build an embankment around you, surround you and close you in on every side, and level you, and your children within you, to the ground; and they will not leave in you one stone upon another, because you did not know the*

time of your visitation" (Lk. 19:42–44).

These heartbreaking prophecies about Jerusalem's destruction were fulfilled when the Romans leveled both the Temple and the city in AD 70, a mere six years after Herod's Temple project was finally completed.[6]

THE QUESTIONS

Apparently, after Jesus had shocked His followers, He walked to the Mount of Olives alone and sat there. Perhaps His disciples were so shaken by His declaration of the Temple's future destruction that they stayed behind to talk among themselves about the implications of what they had just heard. Then four of them (Peter, James, John, and Andrew) went to Jesus privately as He sat on the mount "opposite the Temple" (Mk. 13:3).

They wanted to ask Jesus two questions:

First, "Tell us, when will these things be?" (Mt. 24:3). Since Jesus' foretelling of the Temple's destruction prompted the question, it is obvious they were asking, "When will all these Temple structures be destroyed?" The Gospel of Matthew does not record an answer to this question.

Second, the disciples asked, "And what will be the sign of Your coming, and of the end of the age?" (v. 3). Perhaps they were thinking the Temple would be destroyed at Christ's Second Coming and the end of the age. This is the big one—the question answered in the Olivet Discourse—and it contains five significant points:

1. The word translated "sign" refers to something visible and distinct that enables those who see it to draw a specific conclusion. A biblical sign is a form of divine verification. It is to confirm the identity of a person, thing, or event.[7] In Matthew 24:3 and other passages, the word means a "sign of things to come" and, therefore, "to be expected."[8] Once that specific sign appears, people can be certain of the imminence of Christ's coming and the end of the age.[9]

2. In the Greek text, the word translated "sign" is singular. Preceding it is the definite article for "the." The combination of the singular number and definite article indicate there will be one specific sign only, not two, for the coming of Christ

and end of the age. Thus Christ's coming and the end of the age will take place simultaneously, not as two separate events.

3. The Greek construction of the disciples' second question, in accord with the Granville Sharp Rule, indicates they understood that Christ's coming and the end of the age would, in essence, be the same event.[10] The Granville Sharp Rule states that if the Greek word *kai* joins two nouns of the same case, and only the first noun is preceded by a definite article, then the two nouns refer to the same subject.

4. The word translated "coming" has two basic meanings: "presence" and "*coming, advent* as the first stage in presence."[11] In Matthew 24:3 and other New Testament passages, the word is used "in a special technical sense . . . of Christ, and . . . his Messianic Advent in glory to judge the world at the end of this age."[12] The fact that this term referred to a future coming of Christ as the first stage in His presence implied that before this coming, there would be a time when He would not be physically present on Earth.

5. The disciples' question revealed their understanding that "the age" would end at this future coming of Christ. Their understanding was based on two beliefs:

   » That the promised Messiah, according to the Hebrew Scriptures and the teaching of Jewish rabbis, would rule this present Earth during the last age of its history.

   » That all of world history is divided into two ages. The rabbis taught that the Messiah will be present to end the first age, with its corrupt governments and evil characteristics, and that He will inaugurate the second age characterized by His worldwide righteous rule, peace, and blessings.

Theologian Gerhard Kittel stated,

Among the Rabbis the two aeons are "this aeon" and "the coming aeon." . . . That the Rabbis understood the two aeons in the temporal sense is shown by the many attempts to integrate the old concept of the last time, "the days of the Messiah," into the framework of the doctrine of two aeons.[13]

The New Testament clearly presents the concept of two ages. On the one hand, it refers to "this present evil age" (Gal. 1:4); calls Satan "the god of this age" (2 Cor. 4:4); speaks of "the wisdom of this age" (1 Cor. 2:6) and the "sons of this age" (Lk. 20:34); and declares that Christians "should live soberly, righteously, and godly in the present age" (Ti. 2:12). On the other hand, it refers to "the powers of the age to come" (Heb. 6:5) and draws a distinction between "this age" and "that which is to come" (Eph. 1:21).

The present era could be called the pre-Messianic Age because it precedes the time when the Messiah will be physically present on Earth, administering God's rule worldwide. The rabbis called the age to come "the Messianic era" and "the age of the Messiah."[14]

Consequently, the essence of the disciples' second question was as follows: What visible, distinct sign will announce with certainty the imminence of Your coming as the Messiah and the end of this age?

THE RESPONSE

The apostle Matthew recorded the Lord's response to this second question. Perhaps, by the time Matthew wrote his Gospel, he understood the Temple's destruction would be totally unrelated to the Messiah's future coming and end of the age.

Remember, the question to which Jesus responded was asked by Jewish believers in a completely Jewish setting. That fact, together with some of the content of Jesus' answer, seems to indicate He responded to His disciples as representatives of Jewish believers who will be part of the generation living at the time of His coming and end of the present age:

> *And Jesus answered and said to them, "See to it that no one misleads you. For many will come in My name, saying, 'I am the Christ,' and will mislead many. You will be hearing of wars and rumors of wars. See that you are not frightened, for those things must take place, but that is not yet the end. For nation will rise against nation, and kingdom against kingdom, and in various places there will be famines and earthquakes. But all these things are merely the beginning of birth pangs* (24:4–8, NASB).

OVERVIEW OF THE SEVEN-YEAR TRIBULATION

Jesus indicated that the time leading up to His coming and end of the Pre-Messianic age will be characterized by "tribulation" (vv. 21–22, 29–30). Consequently, He began His response to the disciples' second question with an overview of the entire Tribulation in chronological order (note verse 14: "and then the end will come"). He divided the period into two sections: the beginning of birth pangs and the hard-labor birth pangs.

THE TWO DIVISIONS OF THE BIRTH PANGS

Seven-Year Tribulation	
Tribulation	Great Tribulation
	Time of Jacob's Trouble
Beginning of Birth Pangs	Hard-Labor Birth Pangs
First Half	Second Half
3 1/2 years	3 1/2 years

It is important to note here that the true, Bible-believing church will already have been removed from Earth "in the twinkling of an eye" via the Rapture, prior to the events Jesus described to His disciples (1 Cor. 15:52). In the revelation Jesus gave to the apostle John approximately 60 years after His resurrection, He declared, "Because you have kept My command to persevere, I also will keep you from the hour of trial which shall come upon the whole world, to test those who dwell on the earth" (Rev. 3:10). That "trial" is the Tribulation.

THE BEGINNING OF BIRTH PANGS

Jesus commanded Jewish believers who will live during the future Tribulation to "take care"[15] that they not let anyone deceive them into believing the Messiah and end of the current age have come (Mt. 24:4). Why? Because certain things must take place first. And the first among those things is "the beginning of birth pangs" (literal translation, v. 8).

Jesus used birth pangs as a metaphor, a figure of speech that suggests a likeness or analogy between two things.

The Bible associates birth pangs with the future Day of the Lord

(Isa. 13:6–13) and the time of Jacob's trouble (Jer. 30:6–7). Based on these and related passages, "The idea [in ancient Judaism] became entrenched that the coming of the Messiah will be preceded by greatly increased suffering.... This will last seven years. And then, unexpectedly, the Messiah will come."[16]

According to Millar Burrows, an authority on the Dead Sea Scrolls and other Jewish literature, "A prominent feature of Jewish eschatology [doctrine of future things], as represented by the rabbinic literature, was the time of trouble preceding Messiah's coming. It was called 'the birth pangs of the Messiah,' sometimes more briefly translated as 'the Messianic woes.'"[17]

Why call these future troubles "the birth pangs of the Messiah"? Because travail precedes birth, and this travail "precedes the birth of a new era"[18]—the Messianic Age. Just as a woman must endure great pain before her child is born, so the world will go through birth pangs before the Messianic Age is born.

According to the ancient Jewish *Apocalypse of Abraham*, these birth pangs will involve such things as the sword (war), famine, pestilence, and wild beasts.[19] It is interesting to note that God called "the sword and famine and wild beasts and pestilence" "My four severe judgments" (Ezek. 14:21). Thus "'birth pangs' are a favorite metaphor for the tribulations God's judgment brings upon man."[20]

Jesus indicated that the beginning of birth pangs will consist of the following:

- Many false messiahs. They will use Jesus' name and say, "I myself am the Messiah" (Mt. 24:5, literal translation).
- Deception. They will deceive many into believing the Messiah and end of the age are already present (v. 5).
- Anti-Semitism. No doubt they will direct their deception primarily toward Jewish people, who will be looking for the coming of the Messiah and the Messianic Age.
- Wars and rumors of wars. Nation will rise up against nation, and kingdom against kingdom (vv. 6–7).
- Famines, pestilences, and earthquakes in various places (v. 7).

Jesus commanded Jewish believers who will live during that time not to become "disturbed" or "frightened"[21] by these things because they are a "necessary"[22] part of God's plans for the future[23] (v. 6). Furthermore, "the end" of the present age "is not yet" (v. 6), and "all these things" are merely "the beginning of sorrows [birth pangs]" (v. 8). Additional birth pangs must occur before the future coming of Christ and end of the age.

So the world will become an extremely difficult, dangerous place in which to live. People will suffer enormously and will suffer even more as the birth pangs grow in intensity.

THE TIME OF THE BEGINNING OF BIRTH PANGS

Jesus presented things in chronological order in His overview of the seven-year Tribulation. He presented the beginning of birth pangs first, placing them in the first three and a half years.

There is also more biblical evidence that the beginning of birth pangs will take place during the first half of the Tribulation, not before it or during the second half.

If you compare Christ's description of the beginning of birth pangs in Matthew 24:5–8 with the first four seal judgments of Revelation 6:1–8, you can see they are the same thing.

Scripture teaches that a sinister, evil man of sin will make his appearance and conquer and rule the world during the Tribulation. He is called the Antichrist because he will be the antithesis of the true Christ and will embody Satan's ultimate attempt to overthrow God.

The fact that the Antichrist has not been revealed yet and is not yet conquering the world indicates no birth pangs have begun. The breaking of the first seal unleashes God's judgment and initiates the beginning of birth pangs by bringing the Antichrist to the foreground.

Beginning of Birth Pangs (Mt. 24)	The First Four Seals (Rev. 6)
1. False messiahs who will mislead many (v. 5).	1. First Seal: rider on white horse, a false messiah (vv. 1–2)
2. Wars, rumors of wars, nation rising against nation (vv. 6–7)	2. Second Seal: rider on red horse; takes peace from the earth (vv. 3–4)
3. Famines (v. 7)	3. Third Seal: rider on black horse; holds scales, represents famine (vv. 5–6)
4. Death through famines, pestilences, and earthquakes (v. 7)	4. Fourth Seal: rider on pale horse; represents death through famine, pestilence, and wild beasts (vv. 7–8).

Immediately after Jesus described the beginning of birth pangs, He warned that people associated with Him will be murdered: "Then they will deliver you up to tribulation and kill you, and you will be hated by all nations for My name's sake" (Mt. 24:9). The fifth seal parallels His words, referring to people killed because of their testimony (Rev. 6:9–11). "When He opened the fifth seal, I saw under the altar the souls of those who had been slain for the word of God and for the testimony which they held" (v. 9).

Ancient Judaism taught that the birth pangs of the Messiah will take place during the seven years prior to the Messiah's coming to usher in the Messianic Age. It also taught that these birth pangs will involve the sword (war), famine, pestilence, and wild beasts. It is interesting that ancient Judaism's concept corresponds to the beginning of birth pangs and the first four seal judgments. So the beginning of birth pangs and the first four seals will occur within the seven years prior to the Messiah's coming.

The Bible also indicates that birth pangs characterize the Day of the Lord (Isa. 13:6–13; Zeph. 1:14–18). The word translated "trouble" in Zephaniah 1:15 is one of the Hebrew words for the pangs of a woman giving birth.[24] And the apostle Paul used the birth-pang metaphor to describe the future Day of the Lord: "For you yourselves know perfectly that the day of the Lord so comes as a thief in the night. For when they say, 'Peace and safety!' then sudden destruction comes upon them, as labor pains upon a pregnant woman" (1 Th. 5:2–3).

Through this metaphor, Paul taught that the destruction at the onset of the future Day of the Lord will come suddenly, without warning, like "the birth pang" (literal translation) of a woman. Paul used the singular form and placed the definite article *the* before it, indicating he was referring to the very first birth pang. It is only a woman's first birth pang that comes suddenly and without warning. Once she has the first, she knows the others are coming. Thus the beginning of the future Day of the Lord will like the first birth pang.

Since the beginning of birth pangs to which Jesus referred in Matthew 24:5–8 must include the first birth pang, and the first pang initiates the Day of the Lord (1 Th. 5:2–3), then the beginning of birth pangs must come at the onset of the future Day of the Lord.

The Day of the Lord involves an outpouring of God's wrath on the ungodly:

> *Wail, for the day of the LORD is at hand! It will come as destruction from the Almighty. . . . Pangs and sorrows will take hold of them; they will be in pain as a woman in childbirth; . . . Behold, the day of the LORD comes, cruel, with both wrath and fierce anger, to lay the land desolate; and He will destroy its sinners from it* (Isa. 13:6, 8–9).

Zephaniah 1:14–15, 18 declares,

> *The great day of the LORD is near; . . . That day is a day of wrath, a day of trouble and distress, a day of devastation and desolation, a day of darkness and gloominess, a day of clouds and thick darkness. Neither their silver nor their gold shall be able to deliver them in the day of the LORD's wrath.*

In his 1 Thessalonians 5 discourse on the future Day of the Lord, the apostle Paul said, "God did not appoint us [the righteous in Christ] to wrath, but to obtain salvation through our Lord Jesus Christ" (v. 9).

God's "four severe judgments" (Ezek. 14:21; cf. 5:17) on the ungodly are "the sword and famine and wild beasts and pestilence" (14: 21). Since these are the types of judgments involved with the beginning of birth pangs and first four seals, they must be instruments of God's wrath in the future Day of the Lord.

The Hebrew words for "tribulation" in the Old Testament and the Greek word for "tribulation" in the Septuagint (the Greek translation of the Hebrew Scriptures that Jesus and the apostles sometimes quoted) and Greek New Testament associate the concept of tribulation with the following:

- Birth pangs (2 Ki. 19:3; Jer. 6:24; Jn. 16:21).
- Sword (war), famine, and pestilence (2 Chr. 20:9; Job 15:20–24; Acts 7:11).
- Removal of peace; nations warring against nations (2 Chr. 15:5–6).

The Bible thereby associates the concept of tribulation with the same types of things included in the beginning of birth pangs of Matthew 24:5–8 and the first four seals of Revelation 6:1–8.

SIGNIFICANCE OF THE EXPRESSION "BEGINNING OF BIRTH PANGS"

Since a woman's beginning birth pangs are followed by severe hard-labor pangs, the metaphor suggests that the first half of the Tribulation will be followed by far worse trouble in the second half.

New Testament scholar Gerhard Delling explained that the word translated "beginning" in the expression "the beginning of birth pangs" indicates "the first occurrence in a series of similar corresponding events."[25] Scholar Georg Bertram wrote, "Seduction, wars, famines and earthquakes are the woes with which the end-time is ushered in, or the beginning of sorrows which will be followed by others that are even more severe."[26]

Thus Jesus began to unfold for His disciples the first three and a half years of the Tribulation, when the first seal of God's judgment will be broken and the beginning of birth pangs will grip the world as the dreadful, awful Day of the Lord gets underway. And so begins the worst time on Earth that mankind will ever know.

CHAPTER 2

Characteristics of the Second Half of the Tribulation

Matthew 24:9–14

Matthew 24:9–14 reveals the characteristics of the second half of the seven-year Tribulation:

Then they will deliver you to tribulation, and will kill you, and you will be hated by all nations because of My name. At that time many will fall away and will betray one another and hate one another. Many false prophets will arise and will mislead [deceive] many. Because lawlessness is increased, most people's love will grow cold. But the one who endures to the end, he will be saved. This gospel of the kingdom shall be preached in the whole world as a testimony to all the nations, and then the end will come [NASB].

Jesus began this statement to His disciples with the word *then*, an adverb of time. In some instances, the word refers to the past; in others, to "what follows in time."[1] Some interpreters of verse 9 believe Jesus used it to refer to what will transpire during the beginning of birth pangs already described in verses 5–7, not to what that will take place afterward.

It seems more likely, however, that He used the word to refer to what follows in time—what will take place *after* the beginning of birth pangs:

First, Jesus' statement "All these are the beginning of sorrows [birth pangs]" (v. 8) incorporates the type of phraseology a speaker uses to indicate he is concluding the subject he has just addressed. It seems to imply He was finished with the subject of the *beginning* of birth pangs and would now address what will take place afterward.

Second, Jesus concluded the next section of His discourse (vv. 9–14) with the comment, "and then the end will come" (v. 14). Since the discourse was the Lord's response to His disciples' question "What will be the sign of Your coming, and of the end of the age?" (v. 3), His declaration "and then the end will come" (v. 14, cf. v. 13) most likely refers to the end of the current pre-Messianic Age, when He will come to Earth to establish the Messianic Age. Since the seven-year Tribulation will be the last segment of the pre-Messianic Age, the events immediately preceding "the end" of that age must include events of the second half of the Tribulation.

SEVERE PERSECUTION OF JEWISH BELIEVERS

Persecution will be brought against everyone who becomes saved throughout the seven-year Tribulation, regardless of religious or ethnic background (Rev. 6:9–11; 7:9–17; 20:4). Remember, the church saints will be gone. They will have been raptured prior to the beginning of birth pangs. Once Satan, God's archenemy, controls and empowers the Antichrist, he will wage war against the Tribulation saints for 42 months (the three and one-half years of the second half of the Tribulation; Dan. 7:21, 25; Rev. 13:4–7).

In the Olivet Discourse, Jesus was speaking to His Jewish disciples as representatives of future Jewish believers in Christ. In doing so, He made it clear that persecution of Jewish believers will be especially severe during the second half of the Tribulation (Mt. 24:9; cf. Rev. 12:6, 13–17). They will be delivered up to "tribulation" ("distress that is brought about by outward circumstances"[2]), killed, and hated by all nations. The construction of the verb form translated "be hated" expresses "the long duration of the hate."[3] The cause of this persecution will be their association with the name of Jesus.

TREMENDOUS GROWTH OF LAWLESSNESS

After the Rapture of the church, the entire world will instantly be plunged into "the apostasy" (literal translation of the Greek text, 2 Th. 2:3): "Let no one in any way deceive you, for it [that Day] will not come unless the apostasy comes first, and the man of lawlessness is revealed, the son of destruction" (NASB).

The word translated "apostasy" or "falling away" means "rebellion, abandonment."[4] In 2 Thessalonians 2:3, it refers to rebellion against God's rule and abandonment to lawlessness.

The Greek text's use of *the* apostasy instead of *an* apostasy indicates this future apostasy will be distinct from past apostasies. It will come suddenly, not gradually over time; and it will be a worldwide, absolute apostasy from the start. Theologian Heinrich Schlier wrote, "In 2 Th. 2:3 *apostasia* is used in the absolute sense as an event of the last days alongside or prior to the appearance of the man of lawlessness. Here a Jewish tradition is adopted which speaks of complete apostasy from God and His Torah shortly before the appearance of the Messiah."[5]

One aspect of "the apostasy" will be the abandonment to lawlessness. Lawlessness involves "a frame of mind" that gives birth to "lawless deeds."[6] Theologian Walter Gutbrod stated that "the inner force" of lawlessness "is probably supplied by a more general sense such as rebellion or revolt against God, or alienation from Him."[7]

Although lawlessness will be prevalent during the first half of the Tribulation, it "will abound" during the second half: "And because lawlessness will abound, the love of many will grow cold" (Mt. 24:12). The verb translated "will abound" means to "increase, multiply."[8] The passive voice here implies a person or things or a combination of the two will exacerbate lawlessness during the second half of the Tribulation.

The Antichrist will be a major cause of this chaotic, degenerate condition. In the middle of the Tribulation, he will seize Israel's new Temple; stop sacrifices and offerings; blaspheme the Almighty; magnify and exalt himself; and set himself up in the Temple, claiming to be God (Dan. 7:25; 9:27; 11:36–37; 2 Th. 2:4; Rev. 13:5–6).

As a great world ruler, he will give humanity the ultimate example of human rebellion against God. He will be the epitome of lawlessness. Satan will empower him to continue this revolt for 42 months (the second half of the Tribulation). It is no wonder 2 Thessalonians 2:3 calls him "the man of lawlessness" (literal translation of the Greek text). Surely, his example will encourage multitudes to defy the true and living God.

In addition, Satan will supernaturally empower the Antichrist to deceive people into worshiping him (vv. 9–11). His satanic methods of enforcement will induce large multitudes into even greater lawless rebellion against God (Rev. 13:4, 7–8, 16–17). Schlier indicated "the power" of the man of lawlessness "increases the apostasy."[9]

LOSS OF CIVILITY AND AFFECTION

However, the second half of the Tribulation will involve more than rebellion against God; it will involve lawlessness against fellow humans. Divine judgments during that time will devastate vast areas of the world (Rev. 7—16). As conditions deteriorate, survival will become increasingly difficult; and people will become exceedingly selfish, abandoning all restraints that hinder their survival.

"And then many will be offended," Jesus said, "will betray one another, and will hate one another" (Mt. 24:10). The noun counterpart of the verb translated "be offended" refers to "that which gives offense" or "causes revulsion, that which arouses opposition, an object of anger" or "disapproval."[10] It relates to the meaning "cause of ruin."[11] As necessities for survival grow scarce and people compete for goods, they will view others as threats to their existence and do whatever it takes to stay alive. Theologian Adolf Schlatter, in his *Kommentarz. Matthausev*, 1929, said Jesus' comments refer "to the numerous actions in which. . . every moral norm is transgressed."[12]

In their desperation, people will hate and betray one another. "The love of many will grow cold" (v. 12). The verb translated "grow cold" means to "go out, be extinguished."[13] Thus Jesus was saying the lawlessness of the second half of the Tribulation will be so profound and pervasive that people will no longer care at all for the welfare of others, not even for that of their own families.

Gustav Stahlin indicated that in Matthew 24:10, Jesus referred to

> *the great tribulation within the Messianic Woes between the beginning of birth pangs (v. 8) and the end (v. 13f). It is not related directly to the wars mentioned just before. Rather the powers of apostasy . . . along with the great tribulation in its many forms (Mt. 24:21) gain the upper hand (cf. Rev. 13:7f., 12–17), subduing both faith and love (v. 10b, 12) in the great majority.*[14]

Stahlin pointed out that Jesus' statement in Matthew 13:41 parallels

His statements in Matthew 24:10, 12 concerning humanity's offensive (*skandalon*) and lawless (*anomia*) actions as people abandon all restraints and fight for survival during the second half of the Tribulation.[15] Matthew 13:40–42 indicates that when Jesus comes from heaven at the end of the present pre-Messianic Age, His holy angels will remove from Earth all these offensive, lawless individuals and cast them into a fiery place of judgment.

THE APPEARANCE OF MANY FALSE PROPHETS

During the second half of the Tribulation, many false prophets "will be raised up" (24:11, literal translation of the Greek text). The passive voice indicates that someone or something will instigate their activity. The fact that they will be "false" prophets implies the instigator is Satan or his demons. The Holy Spirit prompted the apostle Paul to call a false prophet of his time "you son of the devil" (Acts 13:10).

Jesus stated that the false prophets of the last 42 months of the Tribulation will "deceive many" (Mt. 24:11). The verb translated "deceive," with its noun counterpart, refers to people being misled from "the path of truth."[16] One man in particular will be the False Prophet who forces the world to worship the Antichrist upon penalty of death. In Revelation, the apostle John saw him as the beast from the earth:

> *Then I saw another beast coming up out of the earth; and he had two horns like a lamb and he spoke as a dragon. He exercises all the authority of the first beast* [the Antichrist] *in his presence. And he makes the earth and those who dwell in it to worship the first beast. . . . He performs great signs, so that he even makes fire come down out of heaven to the earth in the presence of men. And he deceives those who dwell on the earth because of the signs which it was given him to perform in the presence of the beast, telling those who dwell on the earth to make an image to the beast. . . . And it was given to him to give breath to the image of the beast, so that the image of the beast would even speak and cause as many as do not worship the image of the beast to be killed* (Rev. 13:11–15, NASB).

Theologian Gerhard Friedrich wrote,

False prophets are especially expected in the last days, Mt. 24:11. At
their head is the assistant of antichrist (Rev. 16:13; 19:20; 20:10),
the second beast (Rev. 13:11ff.) which has two horns like a lamb but
speaks like a dragon. . . . He is rather a false prophet because he seduces
men to the false religion of totalitarianism by miracles and brute force.[17]

Through their powers, the False Prophet and his associates will
lead multitudes of Gentiles from the path of truth (Mt. 24:24; Rev.
13:11–17; 16:13–14; 19:20).

False prophets thrive when people struggle to survive and are threatened with death. During the second half of the Tribulation, these
deceivers will offer false hope by claiming they have received special
revelation that promises deliverance and "that they are eschatological
deliverers."[18] When in desperate straits, people will cling to anyone
who offers them hope. It is wise to beware of anyone who claims to
have received special revelation from God.

SALVATION OF THOSE WHO ENDURE TO THE END

In contrast to the false prophets' deceptive messages of hope is Jesus'
true message of hope: "But he who endures to the end shall be saved"
(Mt. 24:13). The verb translated "endures" means to "stand one's ground,
hold out, endure in trouble, affliction, persecution."[19] Jesus was referring
to the true believers who survive the second half of the Tribulation.
Because of their confirmed belief that Jesus the Messiah will return to
establish God's Kingdom on Earth and that the Kingdom is "at hand,"
they will be the ones to stand against the attacks and temptations of
the hostile, unbelieving world.[20] They will stand their ground to "the
end" of the present pre-Messianic Age referred to in Matthew 24:3.

Jesus declared that these believers who remain alive "shall be saved"
(v. 13). They shall be saved in the sense of being delivered at the end
of the pre-Messianic Age, when all the attacks and temptations of the
hostile, unbelieving world end (cf. Jer. 30:7; Dan. 12:1). And they will
enter directly into the Millennial, Messianic Age. This true message
of hope will help believers of that time avoid being deceived by the
Antichrist and false prophets and assure them that the second half of
the Tribulation will not last forever.

THE PREACHING OF THE GOSPEL OF THE KINGDOM

Jesus declared, "And this *gospel of the kingdom* will be preached in all the world as a witness to all the nations, and then the end will come" (Mt. 24:14, italics added).

Many people fail to understand there are two distinct gospels in Scripture: the gospel of the Kingdom and the gospel of 1 Corinthians 15, which could also be called the gospel of Christ. The gospel of the Kingdom says nothing about Christ's death and resurrection. Its content is "repent" because "the kingdom of God is at hand" (Mk. 1:15). By contrast, the gospel the apostle Paul defined in 1 Corinthians 15:1–5 says nothing about the Kingdom of God being at hand. Its entire content is the death, burial, and resurrection of Jesus Christ:

> *For I delivered to you first of all that which I also received: that Christ died for our sins according to the Scriptures, and that He was buried, and that He rose again the third day according to the Scriptures* (vv. 3–4).

In the Olivet Discourse, Jesus indicated that the end of the pre-Messianic Age will come once the gospel of the Kingdom (not the gospel of 1 Corinthians 15) has been preached to all the nations in "the whole inhabited earth."[21]

However, some well-meaning Christians have claimed that neither the Rapture nor Second Coming of Christ can take place until the gospel concerning Christ's death, burial, and resurrection has been preached to all nations. This incorrect assertion frequently arises at missions conferences as an incentive for greater commitment to missions.

While a greater commitment to missions is definitely important, it should not be based on a misunderstanding of Jesus' statement in Matthew 24:14.

THERE ARE SIGNIFICANT DIFFERENCES BETWEEN THE GOSPELS

The gospel of the Kingdom was preached by John the Baptist (3:1–2); Jesus (4:17, 23); and the 12 apostles *before* Jesus' death, burial, and resurrection (4:23; 10:1–7; Mk. 1:14).

The second gospel was defined by Paul and was preached by Paul and the other apostles *after* Jesus' death, burial, and resurrection. Christians preach this gospel today. The two gospels differ dramatically in content, commission, and provision for ministry.

CONTENT

The gospel of the Kingdom was "Repent, for the kingdom of heaven is at hand!" (Mt. 3:1–2; 4:17; cf. 10:7). This gospel said nothing about Jesus' death and resurrection.

Matthew 16:21 indicates that Jesus *began* to reveal to His apostles that He would die and rise again only after they had been preaching the gospel of the Kingdom for a considerable time (since their appointment in Matthew 10).

Although God revealed to the Old Testament prophets both the future death of the Messiah for the sins of the world and His resurrection, the prophets recorded the prophecies without understanding them. In fact, the apostle Peter indicated the prophecies were not for their benefit, but for the benefit of the generations that would live after the Messiah's death and resurrection (1 Pet. 1:9–12).

Since the Messiah's death and resurrection were foretold in the Hebrew Scriptures, those details could have been included in the gospel of the Kingdom. But they were not. Peter reacted strongly to Jesus' statement about His death and resurrection, saying, "Far be it from You, Lord; this shall not happen to You!" (Mt. 16:22). If Peter had already been preaching Jesus' death and resurrection, he would not have reacted that way.

By contrast, the gospel of Christ says nothing about the Kingdom and focuses instead on Jesus' death, burial, and resurrection.

COMMISSION

These two gospels also differed in commission. The gospel of the Kingdom had a *restrictive commission*. Jesus commanded that it be preached exclusively to Israel, not to the Samaritans or Gentiles:

> *These twelve Jesus sent out and commanded them, saying: "Do not go into the way of the Gentiles, and do not enter a city of the Samaritans. But go rather to the lost sheep of the house of Israel. And as you go, preach, saying, 'The kingdom of heaven is at hand'"* (10:5–7).

But the gospel of Christ has a *universal commission*. After He died and rose from the dead, Jesus commanded the apostles to go throughout the world preaching to every creature the gospel Paul defined in 1 Corinthians 15: "He said to them, 'Go into all the world and preach the gospel to every creature'" (Mk. 16:15). "Go therefore and make disciples of all the nations" (Mt. 28:19).

PROVISION FOR MINISTRY

These gospels also differed in provision for ministry. The gospel of the Kingdom involved a *restrictive provision*. Jesus told His followers, "Provide neither gold nor silver nor copper in your money belts, nor bag for your journey, nor two tunics, nor sandals, nor staffs; for a worker is worthy of his food" (10:9–10).

By contrast, the gospel of Christ involved extra provisions and a sword:

> *And He said to them, "When I sent you without money bag, knapsack, and sandals, did you lack anything?" So they said, "Nothing." Then He said to them, "But now, he who has a money bag, let him take it, and likewise a knapsack; and he who has no sword, let him sell his garment and buy one"* (Lk. 22:35–36).

The gospels are different from an important reason: Scripture indicates that for the future Millennial, Davidic Kingdom of God to come to Earth (the Kingdom foretold through the Hebrew prophets), it is Israel, not the Gentiles or Samaritans, that must repent (Zech. 12—14; Acts 3:12–21). That is why the gospel of the Kingdom was to go only to Israel. Israel is to be the spiritual leader of the world in the coming Kingdom (Isa. 2:1–3; 61:6; Zech. 8:20–23).

JESUS SPECIFIED THAT "THIS GOSPEL OF THE KINGDOM" (MT. 24:14) MUST BE PREACHED TO ALL NATIONS BEFORE THE END OF THE PRESENT PRE-MESSIANIC AGE

The use of the descriptive word *this* implies Jesus was referring to the same gospel of the Kingdom that He and His apostles had been preaching up to that point—a gospel that said nothing about His future death and resurrection.

Thus Jesus was stating that the end of the current pre-Messianic Age will come once the gospel of the Kingdom ("Repent, for the kingdom of heaven is at hand!") has been preached to all nations. During the time before Christ's death and resurrection, the gospel of the Kingdom was to be preached exclusively to Israel; but during the second half of the Tribulation, it will be preached to all nations.

Since Jesus' death for the sins of the world and His burial and resurrection, absolutely no one can be saved apart from hearing and believing the gospel of Christ. This fact will be true even during the Tribulation. Therefore, that gospel also must be preached during the Tribulation, but separate from the preaching of the gospel of the Kingdom.

So the question arises, If the gospel of Christ will be preached for people to get saved during that time, then what will be the purpose of preaching the gospel of the Kingdom?

THE GOSPEL OF THE KINGDOM WILL BE PREACHED THROUGHOUT THE WORLD "AS A WITNESS TO ALL THE NATIONS" (V. 14)

The form of the word translated "witness" does not refer to "the evangelistic witness of missionary preaching, which offers the chance of conversion."[22] Instead, it is "a witness for the prosecution against" opponents for the purpose of "proof" of guilt.[23]

Remember, during the second half of the Tribulation, people everywhere will be under the leadership of the Antichrist and working to establish the ultimate form of mankind's rule: a united world kingdom that defies God (Rev. 13:7–8).

The message "Repent, for the kingdom of heaven is at hand!" will warn them that aligning themselves with mankind's united world kingdom makes them guilty of rebellion against God's Kingdom rule that is about to be established over all the inhabited earth. Their kingdom will be destroyed, but God's will last forever (Dan. 2:44; 7:14, 27; Rev. 11:15). Therefore, they should repent.

However, instead of repenting, they will refuse to accept God's rule over the earth (Rev. 9:20–21; 16:10–11). By the end of the Tribulation, they will gather their armies together to try to prevent Jesus from returning to establish God's Kingdom rule (Ps. 2:1–3; Rev. 19:11, 19). It will be Satan's all-out, desperate attempt to dethrone God.

At His Second Coming, however, Jesus will destroy these armed rebels (Ps. 2:9–12; Rev. 19:20–21) and remove all the unsaved from the earth in judgment (Mt. 13:40–42, 49–50; 24:37–41).

WHO WILL PREACH THE GOSPEL OF THE KINGDOM TO ALL THE NATIONS OF EARTH DURING THE SECOND HALF OF THE TRIBULATION?

Probably the 144,000 of Revelation 7:1–8 and 14:1–5.
Seven factors characterize these individuals:

1. All of them will be Jewish (7:4–8), just as the apostles who preached the gospel of the Kingdom were Jewish.
2. All of them will be men (14:3–5, as indicated by masculine gender nouns, pronouns, participles, and adjectives), just as the apostles who preached the gospel of the Kingdom were men.
3. All of them will be redeemed (vv. 3–4).
4. All of them will be celibate (v. 4). None will be married or have family responsibilities. They will be free to go anywhere at any time and to focus all their attention on ministry (cf. 1 Cor. 7:29, 32–33).
5. They will be scattered throughout the world (Rev. 7:1–3). Angels will be commanded to prevent natural disasters from devastating Earth until all these men have been sealed. ("The four corners" and "four winds of the earth" refer to "the whole earth"; cf. Isa. 11:12; Rev. 20:8.)[24]
6. They will be visibly identified with God and Christ (7:3; 14:1). They will be visibly sealed with the names of Jesus and God the Father on their foreheads. A seal is "a means of identification," "a mark which denotes ownership" and "carries with it the protection of the owner."[25] This seal will protect the 144,000 from the trumpet and vial judgments that will wrack the world following the seal judgments, but it will also publicly identify them with the very God and Messiah whose judgment and Kingdom are being preached, thereby make them special objects of the world's hatred (Mt. 24:9).
7. They are called "the servants of our God" (Rev. 7:3).

Who would be better qualified to preach a message throughout the world than Jewish people who are scattered among all the nations and, therefore, know many languages, customs, and cultures?

Possibly the Angel of Revelation 14:6–7.

Then I [John] saw another angel flying in the midst of heaven, having the everlasting gospel to preach to those who dwell on the earth—to every nation, tribe, tongue, and people—saying with a loud voice, "Fear God and give glory to Him, for the hour of His judgment has come; and worship Him who made heaven and earth, the sea and springs of water."

Seven characteristics should also be noted about this angel and his message:

1. He is introduced immediately after the 144,000 in Revelation 14:1–5.
2. Just as the "gospel of the kingdom will be preached in all the world as a witness to all the nations" (Mt. 24:14), so this angel will preach "to those who dwell on the earth—to every nation, tribe, tongue, and people" (Rev. 14:6).
3. He will have a gospel to preach.
4. He will preach from the midst of heaven with a loud voice. As a result, every person on Earth will be able to see and hear him. Thus his preaching will bear witness against all those who do not respond properly.
5. He will preach "an everlasting gospel" (literal translation, v. 6. The definite article *the* in the Greek text is absent.) It is not "*the* gospel" that Paul defined in 1 Corinthians 15, where the Greek definite article is present. The angel's gospel says nothing about Christ's death, burial, and resurrection.
6. His gospel proclaims God as the Creator of the universe, implying His right to judge and rule His creation. Therefore, it commands the world to fear, give glory to, and worship God (Rev. 14:7). This gospel commands people to do what all people since the beginning of time should do in relation to God. No doubt that is why it is called an "everlasting gospel" (v. 6).
7. His gospel explains why people during the second half of the Tribulation should fear, give glory to, and worship God: "For the hour of His judgment has come" (v. 7). The verb used

"is a dramatic aorist expressing a state that is on the point of being realized."[26] Thus, this gospel will warn everyone that "this is the very last chance to change allegiance to the God of heaven" before judgment comes.[27]

This angelic proclamation will substantiate the validity of the preaching by the 144,000.

THE END OF THE AGE

Once the gospel of the Kingdom has been preached to all nations, then, said Jesus, "the end" of the present pre-Messianic Age "will come" (Mt. 24:14). The verb translated "will come" is future tense, but it "has the meaning of a perfect [tense verb]."[28] It thereby emphasizes the permanent ending of the present pre-Messianic Age.

CHAPTER 3

The Time of Jacob's Trouble

Matthew 24:15–21

Some people believe the Tribulation is a New Testament teaching only. But that is not true. In the book of Jeremiah, God foretold an unparalleled time of trouble characterized by birth pangs that will afflict the entire earth. He calls it "the time of Jacob's trouble" (Jer. 30: 7). It will be followed by the Jewish people's return to their homeland from all the countries where they have been scattered; and there, they will serve the Lord and live in peace under a Davidic king (vv. 4–10).

Centuries later Jesus Christ described the same time of trouble, how it will begin, and what will follow it (Mt. 24:15–29). In the Olivet Discourse, He called that time "tribulation."

THE ABOMINATION OF DESOLATION

After Jesus gave an overview of the second half of the Tribulation (vv. 9–14), He used the word *therefore* (v. 15), indicating the next section of His discourse would draw from the characteristics of that future period. Speaking ahead of time to Jewish people who will be living in Judea in the future, He told them to be aware of the event that will launch the second half of the Tribulation: the setting up of the abomination in the Holy Place, as foretold by Daniel the prophet:

> *Therefore when you see the "abomination of desolation," spoken of by Daniel the prophet, standing in the holy place . . . then let those who are in Judea flea to the mountains* (Mt. 24:15–16).

The word *abomination* means "detestable thing." It refers to "anything that must not be brought before God because it arouses His wrath" and is used in the Bible "of everything connected with idolatry."[1]

The Jewish prophet Daniel had written,

> *Then he* [the Antichrist] *shall confirm a covenant with many for one week; but in the middle of the week he shall bring an end to sacrifice and offering. And on the wing of abominations shall be one who makes desolate, even until the consummation, which is determined, is poured out on the desolate* (Dan. 9:27).

Jesus' expression *the holy place* (Mt. 24:15) refers to the Temple. God had commanded Israel to destroy all the idolatrous worship places of the Canaanites and to worship Him exclusively at "the place" where He would place His name and dwell (Dt. 12:1–6, 11), namely, the Temple King Solomon built in Jerusalem (1 Ki. 8:28–30). Jewish people who lived in the first century AD called the Temple "this holy place" (Acts 6:13; 21:28), indicating it was the site reserved for God and His service.[2]

The noun translated "abomination" is neuter in gender, and the verb translated "standing" is perfect tense, indicating the detestable thing is an idolatrous image set up to stand permanently in the Temple. Since (1) the Antichrist will oppose and exalt "himself above all that is called God or that is worshiped, so that he sits as God in the Temple of God, showing himself that he is God" (2 Th. 2:4); and (2) an image of the Antichrist will be made for people to worship (Rev. 13:12–15), it appears the detestable thing set up to stand permanently in the Temple will be an image of the Antichrist.

Daniel 9:27, the prophetic basis of Jesus' Matthew 24:15 statement, foretold that, in the middle of the seven-year Tribulation, the Antichrist "shall bring an end to sacrifice and offering." Evidently, in that future time, Israel will have a Temple in Jerusalem, with a reinstated Old Testament sacrificial system. The Antichrist will end this worship so that he can be worshiped instead of God in Israel's Temple. Daniel 11:36–37 declares,

> *Then the king shall do according to his own will: he shall exalt and magnify himself above every god, shall speak blasphemies against the*

God of gods, and shall prosper till the wrath has been accomplished;
for what has been determined shall be done. He shall regard neither
the God of his fathers nor the desire of women, nor regard any god;
for he shall exalt himself above them all.

The Hebrew language of Daniel 9:27 indicates the Antichrist's activity will be the pinnacle of all the detestable acts ever committed against the Temple in Jerusalem.[3] The worship of this man as God in YHWH's holy place will be more detestable to God than Babylon's destruction of Israel's first Temple (586 BC), the defilement of the second Temple by the demented Seleucid ruler Antiochus Epiphanes (171–165 BC), and Rome's destruction of the second Temple (AD 70).

Since verse 27 discusses the Antichrist's activities, he will be the person to perpetrate the desolation and set up the abomination. Jewish people of that future time should be alert to the positioning of this detestable thing in the Temple, because Daniel 9:24 signifies that every part of this prophecy relates to Israel and Jerusalem: "Seventy weeks are determined for your people and for your holy city." The Antichrist will primarily target the Jewish people.

The Antichrist's action will astonish the people of Israel because, at the beginning of the seven-year Tribulation, he will establish a strong, binding covenant with Israel to protect it from all its enemies for seven years (v. 27). He will operate as the ruler of a revived Roman Empire, consisting of 10 divisions federated together for power in the world (7:2–8, 19–20).

What will provoke the Antichrist to go from being Israel's powerful protector to being its major enemy? Jesus revealed to the apostle John that Satan ("the great dragon . . . that serpent of old, called the Devil and Satan," Rev. 12:9) and his demonic angels will be cast down from heaven to Earth in the middle of the seven years (vv. 7–9). This event will infuriate Satan. Knowing that his time is growing short, he will unleash his full fury on Earth (v. 12).

At that time, Satan will possess the Antichrist and prompt him to stop Israel's Old Testament-style worship of God. Through the Antichrist, he will seize the Temple, establish himself as God in that place, and demand to be worshiped.

Since the Garden of Eden, Satan has fought to usurp God. He craves worship and wants to be worshiped as God (Isa. 14:12–14), and will receive that worship by proxy through his Antichrist:

> *So they worshiped the dragon* [Satan] *who gave authority to the beast* [the Antichrist]; *and they worshiped the beast, saying, 'Who is like the beast? Who is able to make war with him?' And he was given a mouth speaking great things and blasphemies, and he was given authority to continue for forty-two months* (the second three and one-half years of the seven-year Tribulation, Rev. 13:4–5; cf. Dan. 7:25; 12:6–7).

As he receives worship, the Antichrist will blaspheme God:

> *Then he opened his mouth in blasphemy against God, to blaspheme His name, His tabernacle, and those who dwell in heaven. It was granted to him to make war with the saints and to overcome them. And authority was given him over every tribe, tongue, and nation. All who dwell on the earth will worship him, whose names have not been written in the Book of Life of the Lamb slain from the foundation of the world* (Rev. 13:6–8).

In the middle of the seven years, Satan will use his Antichrist to begin his attempt to eradicate Israel. In Revelation 12:13–15, God revealed that Satan will persecute Israel, who is represented as "a woman clothed with the sun, with the moon under her feet, and on her head a garland of twelve stars" (v. 1; cf. vv. 2, 5; Gen. 37:9). Jewish people in Israel will flee to the wilderness for 1,260 days (three and one-half years, Rev. 12:6), where they will be "nourished for a time and times and half a time, from the presence of the serpent [Satan]" (v. 14). Language scholars claim Revelation 12:14 refers to "the apocalyptic time of 1+2+1/2=3 1/2 years, during which according to Daniel 12:7 (cf. 7:25) the Antichrist is to reign on Earth."[4]

Thus Israel will experience unparalleled desolation throughout the entire second half of the Tribulation, as Satan tries to annihilate it. For that reason, God calls this period "the time of Jacob's trouble" (Jer. 30:4–7).

SATAN VS. GOD

At this juncture it is wise to pause for a moment to examine why Satan has such great hatred for Israel and why he will target Israel in particular when he and his demons are cast down to Earth from heaven in the middle of the Tribulation. Satan's goal is to destroy Israel. In fact, he *must* destroy Israel to maintain his control over the world system. To understand the situation, we must look at the biblical events that took place near creation and the cosmic battle Satan has been waging against God.

BEGINNING OF THE SATANOCRACY

In eternity past, God determined to rule over a Kingdom as Sovereign and created the universe to be the realm of His Kingdom. "In six days" God created "the heavens and the earth, the sea, and all that is in them" (Ex. 20:11). He also created two types of personal beings to serve Him in His universal Kingdom.

First, He created a great host of angels to serve Him primarily in the heavenly realm of His Kingdom (Rev. 5:11). Then He created two human beings in His image and likeness to serve Him on Earth (Gen. 1:26). He created them as male and female so they could reproduce, and He gave man dominion over all the earthly province of His universal Kingdom (v. 28). These people were Adam and Eve. They were not storybook characters. They were as real as you and I, and much critical biblical doctrine revolves around their existence.

After God finished creating His Kingdom, He looked at "everything that He had made, and indeed it was very good" (v. 31).

God gave man dominion over the earth, indicating the original form of kingdom government He ordained for the planet was a theocracy—a form in which God is the King, but a representative administers His rule. It was God's will that His rule over Earth be administered by His human representative, Adam.

The government functioned that way for a while. However, some time after God finished creation, the highest-ranked, most magnificent of all His angels became consumed with pride (Ezek. 28:11–17; 1 Tim. 3:6), deceiving himself into thinking he could overthrow God and become "like the Most High" (Isa. 14:12–14). Consequently, God cast this rebellious cherub out of His heaven (Ezek. 28:16) and changed his name to Satan (literally, "Adversary").[5]

Satan disguised himself as a serpent (Rev. 12:9; 20:2), came to Earth, and persuaded humanity to join him in his revolt against God (Gen. 3:13). One of the most tragic consequences of the fall of man was that the theocracy—the original, God-ordained form of kingdom government for Earth—was lost. And Satan, God's ultimate enemy, snatched the rule of the world system away from God's representative and replaced the theocracy with a "satanocracy" (vv. 1–19).

The Bible provides evidence of this radical change:

- When Satan tempted Jesus, he had the authority to cause all the world's kingdoms to pass in visionary form before the Lord and to offer the rule of those kingdoms to whomever he wished. Satan told Christ he had that authority because the rule of the world system had been delivered to him (Lk. 4:5–6). Adam is the one who delivered it when he defected from God.
- Jesus called Satan "the ruler of this world" (Jn. 12:31; 14:30; 16:11).
- Paul called Satan "the god of this age" (2 Cor. 4:4).
- The apostle John declared, "The whole world lies under the sway of the wicked one" (1 Jn. 5:19).

Satan desperately wants to become the ultimate Sovereign of the universe. But there can be only one ultimate Sovereign, and He is God. So Satan has sought to overthrow God and usurp His position.

To accomplish that goal, he began to wage war against God. Because God had used a human representative (Adam) to administer His sovereign rule of the earth, Satan persuaded Adam to defect to him.

This was one of Satan's many attacks in his war against God throughout history. His continuing warfare is the key to discerning the ultimate purpose of world history. Satan's objective is to overthrow God and usurp His place permanently. God's objective (and, therefore, the ultimate purpose) is to glorify Himself by demonstrating that He alone is the ultimate Sovereign.

END OF THE SATANOCRACY

Scripture reveals that to fulfill His purpose for history, God must do at least two things before the history of this present Earth ends.

GOD MUST CRUSH SATAN

He must rid the earth of him and his world-system rule before Earth's history comes to an end, or else God's enemy would defeat Him within the scope of the present earth's history.

In light of this need to crush Satan, we must note a significant fact. Immediately after Satan got Adam to defect, God informed His enemy that the woman's "Seed" would "bruise" his "head" (Gen. 3:15). The word translated "bruise" means "crush."[6] God used language that fit the serpent-form Satan took when he tempted humanity to defect from God. If a human being steps heavily with his heel on a snake's head, he will crush the head and kill the snake.

Consequently, God indicated that, in the future, a human offspring of a woman would do God's work of crushing Satan. Later, God revealed that the person would be His Son, the Messiah ("His Annointed," Ps. 2:2, 7–9; cf. Isa. 11:4; Zech. 14:2–3, 12–15).

GOD MUST RESTORE HIS OWN THEOCRATIC KINGDOM ON EARTH

Because Earth began with God's theocracy as its government, it must also end with God's theocracy as its government. Otherwise, Satan would defeat God within the scope of the present earth's history. Restoring God's Kingdom for earth's final age of history is essential to fulfill God's purpose for the world.

Thus, before this Earth's history ends, God must again have a man— an Adam—functioning as His representative, administering His rule over this earthly theocracy. In the Old Testament, God revealed this Man's identity. He would be

- God's Son and the Messiah (Ps. 2:2, 7; Prov. 30:4).
- God's King who will rule the whole earth (Ps. 2:6, 8; Zech. 14:9).
- A male child born into the world (Isa. 9:6–7).
- A biological descendant of King David (v. 7; Jer. 23:5).
- The "Son of Man" (Dan. 7:13–14).

These facts indicate that, in order to become the future Adam, God's Son would be incarnated in human flesh. Paul referred to Jesus as "the last Adam" (1 Cor. 15:45).

The first Adam lost God's theocratic-Kingdom rule; and Jesus Christ, the last Adam, will restore it by crushing Satan's revolt (Heb. 2:14; 1 Jn.

3:8). He will unleash judgments on Satan's world system (Rev. 6—18), destroy that system's human leaders and military forces (19:11–21), remove all the human members of Satan's kingdom (Mt. 13:36–43, 47–50), and imprison Satan in the bottomless pit (Rev. 20:1–3).

Then the Messiah will restore God's theocratic Kingdom and, as God's representative, administer His rule over this earthly province of God's universal Kingdom for the last age of earth's history (vv. 4–6), which will consist of 1,000 years (v. 4).

Thus God's theocratic Kingdom will be restored for the last millennium (*mille* is Latin for "one thousand"; *annus* is Latin for "year") of our present earth's history. This is why the theocratic Kingdom is often called the Millennial Kingdom.

ISRAEL'S KEY ROLE IN THE RESTORATION OF GOD'S THEOCRATIC KINGDOM

God has appointed Israel to fulfill a key role in ridding Earth of Satan's rule and restoring God's theocratic-Kingdom rule for the last 1,000 years of Earth's existence. Consequently, Satan will make Israel his number one target for annihilation when he and his demonic angels are cast down to Earth in the middle of the Tribulation. He must destroy Israel to prevent God's plans from coming to pass. Satan's failure to do so (and fail he will) spells his own destruction.

Before Israel can function as God intends, it must first repent of its rebellion against God and be reconciled to its Messiah (Zech. 12—14; Acts 3:12–21). For that reason, John the Baptist told the people of Israel, "Repent, for the kingdom of heaven is at hand" (Mt. 3:1–2). And, for that reason, Jesus preached to the Jewish people, "Repent, for the kingdom of heaven is at hand" (4:17). He "went about all Galilee, . . . preaching the gospel of the kingdom" (v. 23).

God's theocratic Kingdom was at hand at that time because Jesus Christ, the Messiah, was present. He could have restored it then, if Israel had turned from its rebellion against God and accepted Jesus as its Messiah.

That is why Jesus gave His 12 apostles the restrictive commission, "Do not go into the way of the Gentiles, and do not enter a city of the Samaritans. But go rather to the lost sheep of the house of Israel. And as you go, preach, saying, 'The kingdom of heaven is at hand'" (10:5–7). On one occasion Jesus said, "I was not sent except to the lost sheep of the house of Israel" (15:24).

It is exclusively the nation of Israel, not the Gentiles or Samaritans, that must meet the spiritual requirement of repentance toward God in order for God to crush Satan forever, rid the world system of Satan's rule, and restore His theocratic-Kingdom rule.

Satan knows the Bible well. He does not dare allow Israel to repent because he knows it means his defeat. He will lose control of the world system and be confined in judgment eternally. Thus he will focus his attention on destroying Israel throughout the second half of the Tribulation.

When God unleashes the next-to-the-last Tribulation judgment, Satan, the Antichrist, and the False Prophet will send out miracle-performing demons to prompt the rulers of all nations to deploy their armies to Israel for "the battle of that great day of God Almighty" (Rev. 16:12–14; 19:19–21). Satan's strategy is to use the world's combined military might to eliminate Israel before it repents and welcomes its Messiah. Zechariah 13:8 foretells that two-thirds of the Jewish people living in their homeland at that time "shall be cut off and die, but one-third shall be left in it."

Jesus deeply loves the Jewish people. No wonder why, in His Olivet Discourse, He forewarned those who will be in Israel at that time:

> *"Therefore when you see the 'abomination of desolation,' spoken of by Daniel the prophet, standing in the holy place" (whoever reads, let him understand), "then let those who are in Judea flee to the mountains. Let him who is on the housetop not go down to take anything out of his house. And let him who is in the field not go back to get his clothes. But woe to those who are pregnant and to those who are nursing babies in those days! And pray that your flight may not be in winter or on the Sabbath. For then there will be great tribulation, such as has not been since the beginning of the world until this time, no, nor ever shall be" (Mt. 24:15–21).*

GOD'S GOAL

Although Satan will move the world's armies against Israel, God also will play a role in the maneuver:

Behold, the day of the LORD is coming, and your spoil will be divided
in your midst. For I will gather all the nations to battle against
Jerusalem; the city shall be taken, the houses rifled, and the women
ravished. Half of the city shall go into captivity, but the remnant of
the people shall not be cut off from the city (Zech. 14:1–2).

God will have a twofold purpose, one of which will be to rescue
Israel and destroy the armies.

GOD'S FIRST PURPOSE WILL BE TO BRING THE ONE-THIRD REMNANT OF JEWISH
PEOPLE LEFT IN THEIR HOMELAND TO REPENTANCE AND RECONCILIATION WITH
THEIR MESSIAH AND SAVIOR:

I will bring the one-third through the fire, will refine them as silver
is refined, and test them as gold is tested. They will call on My name,
and I will answer them. I will say, "This is My people"; and each one
will say, "The LORD is my God" (13:9).

When it became obvious the majority of Israel would reject the
Messiah during His First Coming, Jesus lamented,

O Jerusalem, Jerusalem, the one who kills the prophets and stones
those who are sent to her! How often I wanted to gather your children
together, as a hen gathers her chicks under her wings, but you were
not willing! See! Your house is left to you desolate; for I say to you,
you shall see Me no more till you say, "Blessed is He who comes in the
name of the LORD!" (Mt. 23:37–39).

In the Jewish people's darkest hour, as armies attack the remnant
left in Jerusalem, they will realize their only hope of survival is for God
to send the Messiah who comes in the name of the Lord.

In response to their cry for the Messiah, Jesus will descend to Earth
at His Second Coming. Zechariah 12:10 declares, "They will look on
Me whom they pierced. Yes, they will mourn for Him as one mourns
for his only son, and grieve for Him as one grieves for a firstborn."

When they see the glorified Savior descending from heaven with
the wounds of His crucifixion in His resurrected body, they will finally
understand who He is, repent (change their minds about Him), and

accept Him as their Messiah.

According to the Hebrew Scriptures, "In that day a fountain shall be opened for the house of David and for the inhabitants of Jerusalem, for sin and for uncleanness" (13:1). God "will say, 'This is My people'; and each one will say, 'The Lord is my God'" (v. 9).

The prophet Daniel, more than 500 years before the Messiah's First Coming, prophesied concerning this event. God revealed to him that when the Antichrist takes control of Jerusalem in the middle of the Tribulation (Dan. 11:45), the archangel Michael, who serves as the guardian angelic prince of the nation of Israel (10:21; 12:1), will wage an all-out war to prevent Israel's annihilation (12:1). Daniel was told why that will be necessary: "And there shall be a time of trouble, such as never was since there was a nation, even to that time. And at that time your people shall be delivered, every one who is found written in the book" (v. 1).

After that revelation, Daniel saw three personal beings. One had appeared to Daniel in chapter 10 to begin revealing future events. He is described as the "man clothed in linen," who stood above the Tigris River. Apparently he had the form of a man, but his body "was like beryl, his face like the appearance of lightning, his eyes like torches of fire, his arms and feet like burnished bronze in color, and the sound of his words like the voice of a multitude" (10:5–6). Some scholars believe this may have been the pre-incarnate Christ.

Scholars believe the other two beings were angels. One of them asked the man in linen, "How long shall the fulfillment of these wonders be?" (12:6). This angel wanted to know how long the Antichrist will persecute Israel after he breaks his covenant with that nation.[7]

In response to the angel's question, the man in linen held both his hands up to heaven and swore an oath by God. Usually, only one hand is raised in the swearing of an oath. The fact that the man raised both hands emphasized the oath's solemnity and importance.[8] The fact that he invoked an oath based on the eternal God, who is sovereign and truthful, asserts the truthfulness and reliability of his answer, which was twofold:

First, he swore that the Antichrist will be able to persecute Israel "for a time and times and half a time," or three and one-half years (Dan. 7:25; Rev. 12:14; cf. Rev. 11:2; 12:6; 13:5). This persecution will take place during the latter three and one-half years of the Tribulation, the 70th period of seven years of God's program for Israel. (See Daniel 9:24–27 for Daniel's 70-weeks prophecy, where each "week" represents seven years.)

Second, the man clothed in linen indicated that the Antichrist's persecution of Israel will last until Israel's rebellion ceases at the end of the 70th "week" at the Messiah's Second Coming. At that time, Israel will recognize the Messiah and believe in Him. In other words, the man clothed in linen was promising with a solemn oath that the Antichrist's oppression of Israel will last only until it accomplishes its sovereignly designed purpose: until "the power of the holy people has been completely shattered" (Dan. 12:7), and Israel is humbled and reconciled to God.

GOD'S SECOND PURPOSE FOR BRINGING THE ARMIES OF ALL THE NATIONS AGAINST ISRAEL IS TO DESTROY THOSE FORCES AND THEIR LEADERS:

> *Behold, I will make Jerusalem a cup of drunkenness to all the surrounding peoples, when they lay siege against Judah and Jerusalem. And it shall happen in that day that I will make Jerusalem a very heavy stone for all peoples; all who would heave it away will surely be cut in pieces, though all nations of the earth are gathered against it. It shall be in that day that I will seek to destroy all the nations that come against Jerusalem* (Zech. 12:2–3, 9).

Once the remnant of Israel welcomes its Messiah and is cleansed, God "will go forth and fight against those nations" (14:3). He will destroy the nations' armies and leaders and cast the Antichrist and False Prophet into the Lake of Fire (vv. 12–15; Rev. 19:11–21). And Satan will be bound and imprisoned in the bottomless pit for 1,000 years (Rev. 20:1–3).

THE RESTORATION OF GOD'S THEOCRATIC KINGDOM DEPENDS ON ISRAEL'S REPENTANCE AND RECONCILIATION.

Over the years, many Jewish people have wondered what in the world God has chosen them for. Because of the horrible persecutions they have suffered at the hands of organized Christendom, it is not unusual for them to joke, "I wish God had chosen someone else!"

Satan, of course, who has spearheaded the persecutions, wants to make sure the church continues to persecute them because it drives them farther away from the truth of God's love for them, demonstrated at Calvary.

Yet the Jewish people are, and forever will be, God's Chosen People. As Moses told them, "The LORD your God has chosen you to be a people for Himself, a special treasure above all the peoples on the face of the earth" (Dt. 7:6). In the future, God has a magnificent mission for Israel: The nation will be the spiritual head of His coming Messianic Kingdom. But that position cannot be realized until His Chosen People are reconciled with their Messiah.

ISRAEL'S ELECTION

When God delivered Israel from its 400 years of slavery in Egypt and brought the Israelites to Mount Sinai, He revealed two purposes for the nation: to be (1) a holy nation and (2) a kingdom of priests: "You shall be to Me a kingdom of priests and a holy nation" (Ex.19:6). "Holy" means "to divide."[9] God divided Israel from all other nations by making it His exclusive possession. It was to be dedicated exclusively to Him.[10]

Moses told the Israelites, "You are a holy people to the LORD your God; the LORD your God has chosen you to be a people for Himself, a special treasure above all the peoples on the face of the earth" (Dt. 7:6). Years later, David said to God,

And who is like Your people, like Israel, the one nation on the earth whom God went to redeem for Himself as a people, to make for Himself a name—and to do for Yourself great and awesome deeds for Your land—before Your people whom You redeemed for Yourself from Egypt, the nations, and their gods? For You have made Your people Israel Your very own people forever; and You, LORD, have become their God (2 Sam. 7:23–24).

At Mount Sinai, God revealed His second purpose for Israel: to make the nation "a kingdom of priests" (Ex. 19:6). God ordained Israel to be the spiritual leader of the world.

Centuries earlier, Gentile nations had rejected belief in the true and living God. They worshiped their invented images of nonexistent gods and goddesses and followed evil practices. Much of their worship involved sacrificing people by burning them alive or cutting out their hearts. In contrast, God told Israel,

> *"You are My witnesses," says the LORD, "and My servant whom I have chosen, that you may know and believe Me, and understand that I am He. Before Me there was no God formed, nor shall there be after Me. I, even I, am the LORD, and besides Me there is no savior"* (Isa. 43:10–11).

ISRAEL'S FAILURES

The Hebrew Scriptures tell extensively of Israel's failure to fulfill its God-ordained purposes. Furthermore, since God met with the nation at Mount Sinai, history has shown that many Jewish people have rejected belief in the true and living God. Some have accepted belief in pagan gods; some have become agnostic or atheistic; and others devote themselves to the Torah and rabbinical writings but ignore the Old Testament prophets. And the only Jewish people who accept the New Testament are Jewish believers in Jesus.

As a result of Israel's failure to be the God-ordained spiritual leader of the world, it has been conquered by Gentile nations, scattered from its homeland, and subjected to genocide and threats.

ISRAEL'S ELEVATION

Nevertheless, the true and living God of the Bible loves Israel deeply and still intends for it to play a key role in the future theocratic Kingdom.

The restoration of that Kingdom depends on Israel's repentance and acceptance of its Messiah precisely because God has ordained that nation to be the spiritual leader of the world throughout His 1,000-year theocratic-Kingdom.

The following passages indicate Israel's leadership position in the Millennial Kingdom:

> *The word that Isaiah the son of Amoz saw concerning Judah and Jerusalem. Now it shall come to pass in the latter days that the mountain of the LORD's house shall be established on the top of the mountains, and*

*shall be exalted above the hills; and all nations shall flow to it. Many people shall come and say, "Come, and let us go up to the mountain of the L*ORD*, to the house of the God of Jacob; He will teach us His ways, and we shall walk in His paths." For out of Zion shall go forth the law, and the word of the L*ORD *from Jerusalem. He shall judge between the nations, and rebuke many people; they shall beat their swords into plowshares, and their spears into pruning hooks; nation shall not lift up sword against nation, neither shall they learn war anymore* (Isa. 2:1–4).

This passage indicates that the Millennial Temple is where the Messiah will be located on a high elevation in Jerusalem. People from all nations shall travel to Jerusalem to be taught God's Word and theocratic law by Him. There He will settle issues between the nations and rebuke many people for their wrong actions. As a result, weapons will be transformed into tools of peace, and there will be no wars. Clearly, Israel's capital city, Jerusalem, will be the governmental and spiritual center of the entire world.

*Strangers shall stand and feed your flocks, and the sons of the foreigner shall be your plowmen and your vinedressers. But you shall be named the priests of the L*ORD*, they shall call you the servants of our God* (Isa. 61:5–6).

*Thus says the L*ORD *of hosts: "Peoples shall yet come, inhabitants of many cities; the inhabitants of one city shall go to another, saying, 'Let us continue to go and pray before the L*ORD*, and seek the L*ORD *of hosts. I myself will go also.' Yes, many peoples and strong nations shall come to seek the L*ORD *of hosts in Jerusalem, and to pray before the L*ORD*." Thus says the L*ORD *of hosts: "In those days ten men from every language of the nations shall grasp the sleeve of a Jewish man, saying, 'Let us go with you, for we have heard that God is with you"* (Zech. 8:20–23).

CHAPTER 4

The Unparalleled Time of Trouble

Matthew 24:22–28

W e have seen that Satan hates Israel in particular because Israel's survival is the key to his defeat. So in Jesus' overview of the second half of the Tribulation (Mt. 24:9–14), He told the Jewish people what to do. He emphasized that people living in Israel during that time should flee to the mountains (vv. 16–20) because "there will be great tribulation, such as has not been since the beginning of the world until this time, no, nor ever shall be" (v. 21).

THE TRIBULATION'S UNIQUE NATURE

The word translated "great" refers to what is "intense."[1] The word translated "tribulation" communicates the concept of "distress that is brought about by outward circumstances."[2] Those circumstances will involve Satan and his demons being cast down to Earth, Satan taking possession of the Antichrist, and the Antichrist setting up an image of himself in Israel's Temple and demanding that he be worshiped as God.

In Matthew 24:9, the opening word translated "then" introduces a description of the most intense time of suffering during the second half of the Tribulation. This period could be called the hard-labor birth pangs.

Jesus said the distress of this period will be so intense that nothing has compared with it from "the beginning of the world" (the time of creation;[3] see Mark 13:19). Then He added, "no, nor ever shall be" (Mt. 24:21). The double negative is the most decisive way of negating something in the future.[4] Jesus thereby emphasized the absolute impossibility of there ever being anything to equal the last 42 months of the Tribulation.

He then declared, "And unless those days were shortened, no flesh would be saved; but for the elect's sake those days will be shortened" (v. 22).

Some Christians believe that statement implies God will shorten the time to less than its prophesied duration of three and one-half years (42 months, or 1,260 days), as stated in other biblical passages (Dan. 7:25; 12:6–7; Rev. 12:6, 14; 13:5).

But that is incorrect. Jesus meant that in eternity past, God determined to limit the second half of the Tribulation to 1,260 days. In His omniscience, He knew that if He allowed it to go on indefinitely, "no flesh" would survive (Mt. 24:22).

Several factors support this interpretation. The first verb translated "were shortened" (v. 22) is in the Greek aorist tense. Greek language scholar Gerhard Delling explained, "This cannot be a prophetic aorist because of the other tenses in the passage."[5] He wrote,

> *God has already "cut short" the time of the tribulation in Judea. That is, He has made it shorter than it would normally have been in terms of the purpose and power of the oppressors. If He had not done so, even those who prove themselves to be the elect by their faithfulness, and who have been wonderfully kept thus far, would be brought to physical destruction.*[6]

Interestingly, John Calvin interpreted this passage in light of Paul's exposition of Romans 11 and applied it to the remnant of Israel.[7]

The Gospel of Mark more clearly indicates that God determined in eternity past to limit the second half of the Tribulation to 1,260 days:

> *For in those days there will be tribulation, such as has not been since the beginning of the creation which God created until this time, nor ever shall be. And unless the Lord had shortened those days, no flesh would be saved; but for the elect's sake, whom He chose, He shortened the days* (Mk. 13:19–20).

Delling said Mark places greater "emphasis on the fact that for

God," the decision to shorten the second half of the Tribulation to 1,260 days "is already done."[8]

If, during the second half of the seven-year Tribulation, God were to shorten the prophesied duration of three and one-half years, He would violate the integrity of His authoritative Word.

THE TRIBULATION'S UNIVERSAL IMPACT

So far the emphasis has been on Israel's suffering. However, the second half of the Tribulation will be the unparalleled time of trouble, not only for the people of Israel living in their homeland, but also for people all over the world.

For Jewish people, it will be "the time of Jacob's trouble" (Jer. 30:4–7), as Satan, the Antichrist, demons, and all the nations of the world try to eliminate them from the face of the earth.

However, the Gentiles also will suffer greatly. God's judgments, which are divided into seal, trumpet, and bowl judgments in the book of Revelation, will fall upon the entire earth.

Jesus' declaration, "And unless those days were shortened, no flesh would be saved" (Mt. 24:22) means every human being on Earth would be eliminated. The words translated "no flesh" mean "no person, nobody."[9] If this time of unparalleled trouble were allowed to continue indefinitely, no Jews or Gentiles would survive.

AN OPPOSING VIEWPOINT

Before moving on, it seems good to pause here to explain that some Christians do not believe Jesus was referring to a future, worldwide judgment but, rather, to a disaster that would shatter Israel alone a number of decades after most of the nation rejected Him at His First Coming. This view is sometimes called Preterism, derived from the Latin word *praeter*, which means "past."[10]

Preterists believe the Great Tribulation has already happened. They contend it refers to a coming of Christ to judge the generation of Jewish people who heard His teaching and witnessed His miracles but rejected Him as their Messiah and called for His crucifixion. They also claim the judgment occurred when the Roman Empire crushed the Jewish War against Rome that began in the mid-60s AD and destroyed Jerusalem, Herod's Temple, and Israel as a nation-state in AD 70.

For them, that event was the Second Coming of Christ, and they do not believe He will come again to Earth to restore God's theocratic Kingdom. (Many Christians who advocate Preterism also hold to Covenant Theology.)

PRETERISM'S MANY FLAWS

Jesus clearly indicated the second half of the seven–year Tribulation will be a time of unparalleled trouble, not only for Jewish people, but for everyone (Mt. 24:21–22). It will be so bad, in fact, that it will be worse than anything that has transpired as far back as creation—even before the Jewish people came into existence.

This time will be so terrible that, if allowed to continue indefinitely, it would wipe humanity off the earth.[11] Jesus said "no flesh"—not any, Jewish or Gentile—would survive (v. 22). The Bible associates "tribulation" with "the day of wrath and revelation of the righteous judgment of God" (Rom. 2:5–9).

Furthermore, the trouble that occurred in the first century AD was not the worst the world has ever seen:

The destruction in AD 70 was not worse than the Assyrian destruction of the city of Samaria and the northern kingdom of Israel as a nation-state in 722 BC or the Babylonian destruction of Jerusalem, Solomon's Temple, and the southern kingdom of Judah as a nation-state in 586 BC.

Even if Jesus' reference to "all flesh" perishing (Mt. 24:22) were limited exclusively to the Jewish people, the trouble they endured during the first-century Jewish Wars was not worse than what they suffered in the Holocaust of World War II.

Based on the writings of first-century Jewish historian Josephus, it is computed that 1,356,460 Jews were killed in the Jewish War against the Roman Empire that ended in AD 70. By contrast, some 6 million Jewish people were murdered in the Holocaust.

Jesus indicated that "immediately after" the Great Tribulation, cosmic disturbances will rock the universe: "Immediately after the tribulation of those days the sun will be darkened, and the moon will not give its light; the stars will fall from heaven, and the powers of the heavens will be shaken" (v. 29). There is no record of such occurrences in AD 70.

Jesus declared that after the cosmic disturbances, "the sign of the

Son of Man will appear in heaven" (v. 30). There is no record of that happening in AD 70 either.

Jesus also said His coming will take place *after* the Great Tribulation, not *during* it (vv. 29–30).

Scripture teaches that Jesus' coming will be visible: "Behold, He is *coming with clouds*, and *every eye will see Him*, even they who pierced Him. And all the tribes of the earth *will mourn* because of Him" (Rev. 1:7, emphasis added). Matthew 24:30 says, "Then the sign of the Son of Man *will appear* in heaven, and then all the tribes of the earth *will mourn*, and *they will see* the Son of Man coming on the clouds of heaven with power and great glory" (emphasis added).

The Second Coming will be extremely visible. He will appear. *Every* eye will see Him. And there will be no doubt about His identity. There is no record of a visible appearance of Christ during the Jewish Wars.

Jesus indicated that, in conjunction with His coming on the clouds of heaven, He will "send His angels with a great sound of a trumpet" to gather together His elect people from all four directions of the world (v. 31). Neither is there a record of anything like that taking place either during the Jewish Wars from the mid-60s to AD 70 or after AD 70.

So it is entirely reasonable to conclude that Christ's return has yet to occur, and that prior to it, multitudes from all nations will suffer enormously when the powerful judgments of God's wrath are poured out on Earth during the second half of the future Tribulation.

THE BOWL JUDGMENTS

In the book of Revelation, we see that the first judgments to be poured out on the entire world will be the seal judgments, followed by the trumpet judgments, and then the bowl judgments. These clearly will produce extreme and worldwide suffering. The False Prophet, the Antichrist's henchman, will cause "all, both small and great, rich and poor, free and slave, to receive a mark on their right hand or on their foreheads, and that no one may buy or sell except one who has the mark or the name of the beast [the Antichrist], or the number of his name" (Rev. 13:16–17). That mark, however, will seal its recipient's doom.

"Then," wrote the apostle John, "I saw another sign in heaven, great and marvelous, seven angels who had seven plagues, which are the last, because in them the wrath of God is finished. Then I heard a loud voice from the temple, saying to the seven angels, 'Go and pour out on the earth the seven bowls of the wrath of God'" (15:1; 16:1, NASB).

FIRST BOWL

This judgment will unleash "a foul and loathsome sore . . . upon the men who had the mark of the beast and those who worshiped his image" (16:2). The word translated "sore" relates to the category of "abscess" or "ulcer."[12] The word translated "foul" could also be translated "evil, injurious, dangerous," or "pernicious."[13] The word translated "loathsome" could also be translated "painful, virulent, serious."[14]

SECOND BOWL

This judgment will turn the sea into blood (v. 3). Every living sea creature will die. As a result, a major source of food for humanity will be eliminated, and many fishermen will lose their source of income.

THIRD BOWL

This bowl will turn the rivers and springs—the sources of drinking water—into blood (v. 4) and force those who "have shed the blood of saints and prophets" to drink blood (v. 6). The text says, "for they poured out the blood of saints and prophets, and You have given them blood to drink. They deserve it" (v. 6, NASB). A holy angel will proclaim, "Even so, Lord God Almighty, true and righteous are Your judgments" (v. 7).

FOURTH BOWL

This divine judgment will intensify the sun's fire and scorch people with great heat. But instead of repenting before the living God, people will "[blaspheme] the name of God who has power over these plagues; and they [will] not repent and give Him glory" (vv. 8–9).

FIFTH BOWL

This particular judgment will be poured out on the Antichrist's throne, causing his kingdom to become "full of darkness." His subjects will "[gnaw] their tongues because of the pain" (perhaps the pain inflicted on them during the fourth bowl judgment). Yet they will "[blaspheme] the God of heaven because of their pains and their sores, and [will] not repent of their deeds" (vv. 10–11).

SIXTH BOWL

This bowl will be poured out "on the great river, the Euphrates; and its water was dried up, so that the way would be prepared for the kings from the east" (v. 12, NASB).

Approximately 1,800 miles long (the distance from New York City to Denver, Colorado), the Euphrates is the longest river in southwest Asia and one of the most historically significant. It flows from northeastern Turkey through Syria and Iraq, then joins with the Tigris River near Basra, Iraq, and flows to the Persian Gulf.

Drying up this great expanse will create a roadway for the rulers and armed forces of all the Gentile nations, enabling them to march against Israel by the end of the Tribulation, prior to the return of Jesus Christ (vv. 12–14; 19:11–19).

SEVENTH BOWL

This judgment will prompt noises, thunder, lightning, and an earthquake unparalleled in all of world history (16:17–21). It will cause cities of the Gentile nations to collapse and the great city of Jerusalem to be split into three parts (v. 19).[15] Babylon will experience the fierceness of God's wrath. Every island will vanish, and mountains will disappear.

The earthquake will be followed by a storm of gigantic hailstones, weighing "between 108 and 130 pounds" each.[16] As they plummet from the sky, they will cause massive physical damage, wound and kill scores of people and animals, and destroy vegetation and buildings. The damage from the plague of hail will be so great that unrepentant humanity will blaspheme God (v. 21).

WARNING AGAINST FALSE MESSIAHS AND PROPHETS

Jesus warned people who will be living during the Great Tribulation, "If anyone says to you, 'Behold, here is the Christ,' or 'There He is,' do not believe him. For false Christs and false prophets will arise and will show great signs and wonders, so as to mislead, if possible, even the elect" (Mt. 24:23–24, NASB). Pseudo messiahs will perform such convincing fake signs and miracles that, if it were possible, even Jewish believers would be deceived. However, the words translated "if possible" indicate they will not be deceived.

Through the Olivet Discourse, Jesus cautions Jewish believers living during the Great Tribulation not to believe reports that the Messiah is in some hidden location, such as the desert or secret rooms. They should not go looking for Him (v. 26).

The Messiah's future coming will not be hidden or secret (vv. 27–28). It will be glorious, obvious, bright, and visible as lightning: "For as the lightning comes from the east and flashes to the west, so also will the coming of the Son of Man be" (v. 27). Christ's future appearance will illuminate the entire sky. Jesus specifically emphasized "the inescapable visibility and divine suddenness" of His Second Coming (v. 27).[17] Consequently, Revelation 1:7 states, "Every eye will see Him" when He returns.

Even the effects of His Second Coming will inform the whole world that He is present. Under the Antichrist's leadership, the godless rulers and soldiers of all the Gentile nations will have gathered in Israel to try to destroy the Jewish nation and prevent the Messiah's return (Zech. 14:1–3; Rev. 19:19).

When Christ will descend from heaven, an angel standing in the sun will cry "with a loud voice, saying to all the birds that fly in the midst of heaven, 'Come and gather together for the supper of the great God, that you may eat the flesh of kings, the flesh of captains, the flesh of mighty men, the flesh of horses and of those who sit on them, and the flesh of all people, free and slave, both small and great'" (Rev. 19:17–18). The word translated "birds" refers to "every bird that is unclean and detestable (for religious reasons),"[18] including the vulture (Dt. 14:12).

Jesus declared that one of the effects of His Second Coming will be that "wherever the carcass is, there the eagles will be gathered together" (Mt. 24:28). The word translated "carcass" means "corpse, especially of one killed by violence."[19] In this context, the word translated "eagles" has the meaning of "vulture."[20]

At His return, the Messiah will have the Antichrist and False Prophet captured and cast alive into the Lake of Fire burning with brimstone (Rev. 19:20). Then He will rescue Israel, killing all the rulers and soldiers of all the Gentile nations. As a result, "all the birds" will be "filled with their flesh" (v. 21).

The First Event: Great Cosmic Disturbances

Matthew 24:29–30

Before the Messiah returns and the Antichrist and False Prophet meet their doom, four major and powerful events will take place. Jesus presented them in chronological order in Matthew 24:29–30:

> *Immediately after the tribulation of those days* [1] *the sun will be darkened, and the moon will not give its light; the stars will fall from heaven, and* [2] *the powers of the heavens will be shaken.* [3] *Then the sign of the Son of Man will appear in heaven, and* [4] *then all the tribes of the earth will mourn, and they will see the Son of Man coming on the clouds of heaven with power and great glory. And He will send His angels with a great sound of a trumpet, and they will gather together His elect from the four winds, from one end of heaven to the other.*

These events will take place "in those days [plural], after that tribulation" (Mk. 13:24). The Matthew and Mark passages imply these events and the Second Coming will not occur on the same day but, rather, will be spread out over several days.

The first event will be a series of great cosmic disturbances. Immediately after the Great Tribulation, the sun will be darkened, the moon will not shed its light, and the stars will fall from heaven (Mt. 24:29).

ORIGIN OF THE COSMOS

In Matthew 24:21, the word for "world" is a form of the Greek word *cosmos*: "For then there will be great tribulation, such as has not been since the beginning of the world until this time, no, nor ever shall be." The word *cosmos* refers to "the universe conceived as an orderly and harmonious system; contrasted with chaos."[1]

God created the universe as an orderly, harmonious system: "Oh, give thanks to the God of gods! . . . to Him who alone does great wonders, . . . to Him who by wisdom made the heavens, . . . to Him who laid out the earth above the waters, . . . to Him who made great lights, . . . the sun to rule by day, . . .the moon and stars to rule by night" (Ps. 136:2, 4–9).

The fact that God possesses the wisdom, power, and authority to create the sun, moon, and stars means He also has the authority and power to alter them according to His sovereign will. Immediately after the end of the Great Tribulation, God evidently will exercise His authority and power to darken the sun, moon, and stars (Mt. 24:29).

THE DAY OF THE LORD CONCEPT

These future cosmic disturbances are not the only ones mentioned in the Bible. Scripture also records cosmic disturbances that took place during Old Testament times. These past cosmic disturbances shed light on the significance of the future cosmic disturbances. Several Old Testament passages relate such disturbances to the Day of the Lord.

Old Testament language scholar Magne Sæbø described the Day of the Lord concept as follows: "God is Lord of time, not only because He created the constant alternation between day and night, thus laying the foundation for the course of history, but because He also intervenes mightily in the course of history."[2]

Sæbø said the expression "the Day of the Lord" refers to when God "has a time to act, a time to intervene in 'history'; what will take place then, He alone determines."[3] It refers to a time "when He will intervene, from which no one can escape. This 'day' will bring the opposite of what the people hope for from Yahweh, namely disaster ('darkness') rather than deliverance ('light')."[4]

The Day of the Lord "can bring both disaster and deliverance; it can come to both Israel and the 'nations.'"[5]

OLD TESTAMENT EXAMPLES OF THE DAY OF THE LORD AND COSMIC DISTURBANCES

Isaiah 13:1, 4–6, 9–10 foretold God's judgment on Babylon:

The burden against Babylon which Isaiah the son of Amoz saw. . . . The LORD of hosts musters the army for battle. They come from a far country, from the end of heaven—the LORD and His weapons of indignation, to destroy the whole land. Wail, for the day of the LORD is at hand! It will come as destruction from the Almighty. Behold, the day of the LORD comes, cruel, with both wrath and fierce anger, to lay the land desolate; and He will destroy its sinners from it. For the stars of heaven and their constellations will not give their light; the sun will be darkened in its going forth, and the moon will not cause its light to shine.

Ezekiel 29:19; 30:1–3 speak of "the day of the LORD" to refer to Babylon's defeat of Egypt:

Therefore thus says the Lord GOD: "Surely I will give the land of Egypt to Nebuchadnezzar king of Babylon; he shall take away her wealth, carry off her spoil, and remove her pillage.". . . The word of the LORD came to me again, saying, "Son of man, prophesy and say, 'Thus says the Lord GOD: "Wail, 'Woe to the day!' For the day is near, even the day of the LORD is near; it will be a day of clouds, the time of the Gentiles."'"

Ezekiel 32:5–8 speaks of "the day of the LORD" to refer to Egypt's defeat and its effect on Pharaoh:

I will lay your flesh on the mountains, and fill the valleys with your carcass. I will also water the land with the flow of your blood, even to the mountains; and the riverbeds will be full of you. When I put out your light, I will cover the heavens, and make its stars dark; I will cover the sun with a cloud, and the moon shall not give her light. All the bright lights of the heavens I will make dark over you, and bring darkness upon your land.

Amos 5:18–20 uses the phrase to warn of punishment on the

Jewish nations. Amos prophesied for a short time while the kings of the northern kingdom of Israel and southern kingdom of Judah had an alliance lasting for several years. During that time, the wealthy people abused the poor. Amos warned both kingdoms that God would punish them during the Day of the Lord if they did not repent from their unjust behavior:

> *Woe to you who desire the day of the LORD! For what good is the day of the LORD to you? It will be darkness, and not light. It will be as though a man fled from a lion, and a bear met him! Or as though he went into the house, leaned his hand on the wall, and a serpent bit him! Is not the day of the LORD darkness, and not light? Is it not very dark, with no brightness in it?*

Joel 2:1–2 uses the phrase to warn of trembling, darkness, and gloom in Zion:

> *Blow the trumpet in Zion, and sound an alarm in My holy mountain! Let all the inhabitants of the land tremble; for the day of the LORD is coming, for it is at hand: a day of darkness and gloominess, a day of clouds and thick darkness, like the morning clouds spread over the mountains.*

Joel 3:14–15 speaks of cosmic disturbances in the "valley of decision": "Multitudes, multitudes in the valley of decision! For the day of the LORD is near in the valley of decision. The sun and moon will grow dark, and the stars will diminish their brightness."

THE GREAT DAY OF THE LORD

Four biblical passages use the descriptive term *great* in reference to the Day of the Lord. Joel 2:10–11 and Zephaniah 1:14–15 describe the two historic great Days of the Lord, and Joel 2:30–31 and Malachi 4:5 describe the two future great Days of the Lord. The other Day-of-the-Lord passages do not use that term.

THE PAST

Joel 2:10–11 refers to one of the historic great Days of the Lord. "The earth quakes before them, the heavens tremble; the sun and moon grow dark, and the stars diminish their brightness. The LORD gives voice before His army, for His camp is very great; for strong is the One who executes His word. For the day of the LORD is great and very terrible; who can endure it?"

The Hebrew word translated "great" in describing the Day of the Lord is *gadhol*. Old Testament language scholar R. Mosis explained,

> *When* gadhol *is used to describe an event, it means that that event goes beyond the ordinary and usual. Here, then,* gadhol *indicates that an event is not in the stream of the usual course of history, but breaks into it, interrupts it, or goes beyond it.* Gadhol *has this meaning especially when it is used in connection with those events that are due to God's activity.*[6]

The word translated "very" in conjunction with the word translated "terrible" means "extremely."[7] This description indicates that the Day of the Lord would be extremely terrible for those alive during that time. Its horror prompts the question, "Who can endure it?"[8] Those present during this Day of the Lord would experience "an inward shock,"[9] being overwhelmed by the Lord's unique wisdom, power and authority.

Zephaniah 1:14–15 describes the other historic great Day of the Lord: "The great day of the LORD is near; it is near and hastens quickly. The noise of the day of the LORD is bitter; there the mighty men shall cry out. That day is a day of wrath, a day of trouble and distress, a day of devastation and desolation, a day of darkness and gloominess, a day of clouds and thick darkness."

The contexts of both Joel 2:10–11 and Zephaniah 1:14–15 seem to indicate they refer to the judgments God was planning to bring on the kingdom of Judah in Old Testament times because of its rebellion against Him.

THE FUTURE

Two passages—Joel 2:30–31 and Malachi 4:5—indicate there will be a future Day of the Lord, distinct from all other Days of the Lord.

In Joel 2:30–31, God declared, "And I will show wonders in the heavens and in the earth: blood and fire and pillars of smoke. The sun shall be turned into darkness, and the moon into blood, before the coming of the great and awesome day of the LORD."

This passage corresponds with Jesus' description of that day in the Olivet Discourse. It states that the cosmic darkening of the sun and moon will take place *before* the coming of the great and awesome Day of the Lord. The word translated "before" denotes "a change in the course of an event or act, the beginning of an action, a purposeful orientation. ... that someone or something 'turns.' The subsequent text describes or reveals the result and consequences."[10]

This meaning seems to imply that the cosmic disturbances related to the previous Days of the Lord began when those Days of the Lord began, *not beforehand.* By contrast, *before* God unleashes His future Day-of-the-Lord wrath on the earth, He will cause a "turn" in the orientation of the cosmic disturbances. Instead of beginning *when* that future Day of the Lord begins, they will begin *before* it.[11]

All other biblical texts related to the Days of the Lord—except for Joel 2:30 and Malachi 4:5—do not state that the cosmic disturbances will begin *before* the Days of the Lord. Thus Joel 2:30–31 clearly indicates that the great and awesome Day of the Lord will *follow* the cosmic disturbances.

In addition to being great, the Day of the Lord will be awesome. The word translated "awesome" is *yare.*[12] *Yare* and other Hebrew words describe "the terrifying effect of God on the individual"[13] and "the divine terror that befalls the foe."[14] The event will cause God's enemies to "tremble in panic" and "be shaken" in the presence of deity.[15] It "will incite fear of God's eschatological day of judgment."[16]

Joel 2:30–31 declares that cosmic disturbances will take place *before* the "coming of the great and awesome day of the LORD."

In Matthew 24:29–30, Jesus stated,

Immediately after the tribulation of those days the sun will be darkened, and the moon will not give its light; the stars will fall from heaven, and the powers of the heavens will be shaken. Then the sign of the Son of Man will appear in heaven, and then all the tribes of the earth will mourn, and they will see the Son of Man coming on the clouds of heaven with power and great glory.

So cosmic disturbances will begin *before* Jesus comes out of heaven. Between the beginning of the cosmic disturbances and Jesus' Second Coming to Earth, the powers of the heavens will be shaken, His sign will appear in heaven, all the tribes of the earth will mourn, and finally they will see Him coming with power and great glory.

Christ's Second Coming to Earth will certainly be "great." It will interrupt and go beyond the ordinary course of history. His coming will also be "awesome." It will terrify God's enemies. They will "tremble in panic" and "be shaken" in the presence of deity. They will fear His "eschatological day of judgment."

Consequently, Joel 2:30–31 and Matthew 24:29–30 refer to the same future Day of the Lord.

Malachi 4:5 is the second biblical passage that indicates there is a future Day of the Lord that will be distinct from all others: God declared, "Behold, I will send you Elijah the prophet before the coming of the great and dreadful day of the LORD."

The Hebrew word translated "great" is identical to the word translated "great" in Joel 2:31, and the word translated "dreadful" is identical to the word translated "awesome" in Joel 2:31. This sameness indicates that these two passages refer to the same future Day of the Lord.

Therefore, Malachi 4:5 also refers to Jesus' Second Coming to Earth after the end of the Great Tribulation.

IDENTIFICATION OF THE ELIJAH OF MALACHI 4:5

Since the day of the Lord in Malachi 4:5 refers to the Messiah's Second Coming, God apparently will send Elijah to Earth during the Great Tribulation before Jesus returns. H. P. Muller, an Old Testament language scholar, wrote, "Before the eschatological Day of Yahweh, according to Mal. 3:23f. (4:5f.), the prophet Elijah will return in Israel to preach repentance and reorient the people."[17]

So will God send the same Jewish prophet whom He brought up to heaven in whirlwind when a chariot of fire appeared (2 Ki. 2:11), or will He send someone else? To answer that question, it is necessary to look at the book of Revelation.

ELIJAH IN THE BOOK OF REVELATION

The Revelation of Jesus Christ is the most significant book of the Bible that provides specific information concerning events that will transpire during the Great Tribulation before Christ's Second Coming. Since Malachi 4:5 prompts the conclusion that God will send Elijah to Earth during the Great Tribulation before Christ returns, one would expect Revelation to refer specifically to "Elijah the prophet." But the name Elijah appears nowhere. That fact, however, does not imply that Elijah is not present in Revelation's prophecy. Jesus' comments in the Gospel of Matthew concerning Elijah seem to parallel Revelation's description of two men who will be bold witnesses for Christ during the Tribulation:

> *"And I [Jesus] will grant authority to my two witnesses, and they will prophesy for twelve hundred and sixty days, clothed in sackcloth." And if anyone wants to harm them, fire flows out of their mouth and devours their enemies; so if anyone wants to harm them, he must be killed in this way. These have the power to shut up the sky, so that rain will not fall during the days of their prophesying; and they have power over the waters to turn them into blood, and to strike the earth with every plague, as often as they desire* (Rev. 11:3, 5–6, NASB).

In Old Testament times, God worked through Moses and Elijah to perform supernatural feats. For example, He administered plagues on Egypt through Moses, one of which involved turning water into blood (Ex. 7:14–21). And God enabled Elijah to declare a drought on the northern kingdom of Israel for three and one-half years (1 Ki. 17—18; Lk. 4:25; Jas. 5:17–18). In addition, He twice enabled Elijah to call fire down from heaven to consume more than 50 soldiers whom a wicked king had sent to capture the prophet (2 Ki. 1:8–12).

When Jesus went up to a high mountain, Moses and Elijah appeared with Him (Mt. 17:1–9). Jesus told His apostles, "Assuredly, I say to you, there are some standing here who shall not taste death till they see the Son of Man coming in His kingdom" (16:28). Six days later, He fulfilled that promise when He took three of His disciples (Peter, James, and John) with Him up the mountain and "was transfigured before them. His face shone like the sun, and His clothes became as white as the light" (17:2).

Moses and Elijah then appeared, spoke with Jesus, and later disappeared. A bright cloud overshadowed those left on the mountain, "and suddenly a voice came out of the cloud, saying, 'This is My beloved Son, in whom I am well pleased. Hear Him!'" After the apostles heard God the Father's claim concerning Jesus, "they fell on their faces and were greatly afraid" (vv. 3–6).

In light of what Jesus had said six days earlier, it seems obvious that His transfiguration was a preview of how He will look when He returns to establish His Kingdom with God the Father's approval at the end of the Great Tribulation. That dramatic experience on the mountain must have confirmed the apostles' belief that Jesus was the promised Messiah. But when they came down from the mountain, it prompted them to ask Jesus why the scribes said Elijah must come first (v. 10). The Jewish scribes had taught that Elijah must come before the Messiah will restore God's Kingdom rule.

Jesus provided a twofold answer: "Indeed, Elijah is coming first and will restore all things. But I say to you that Elijah has come already, and they did not know him" (vv. 11–12). The apostles understood that the Elijah who had come already was John the Baptist (v. 13; cf. Mt. 11:11–14; Mk. 1:1–4).

But Jesus indicated there is another Elijah who "is coming first and will restore all things" (Mt. 17:11). John the Baptist himself confirmed he was not that other Elijah when the Jews sent priests and Levites from Jerusalem to ask him, "Are you Elijah?"

He answered, "I am not" (Jn. 1:21).

The fact that Moses and Elijah were the only two men who appeared with Jesus in the preview of the Son of Man coming in His Kingdom, coupled with the fact that God used Moses and Elijah to perform supernatural feats in Old Testament times, seems to imply a significant correlation with the two witnesses in Revelation 11.

The two witnesses will prophesy for 1,260 days (Rev. 11:3) while the Gentiles trample Jerusalem underfoot for 42 months (v. 2) during the second half of the Tribulation before Jesus returns to establish God's Kingdom on Earth. When someone tries to hurt them, fire will shoot from their mouths and kill the enemy. They will turn water to blood, strike the earth with plagues, and bring droughts until the days for them to prophesy are completed. Then they will be killed. Their bodies will lie in the streets of Jerusalem for three and a half days, after which they will come alive and ascend to heaven in a cloud in plain sight

(vv. 6, 11–12). These two witnesses will be prophets ("they will prophesy," v. 3). Both Moses (Dt. 18:15; 34:10–12) and Elijah (1 Ki. 18:22, 36) were exceptional prophets of God. The fact that they will be empowered to do the same supernatural feats Moses and Elijah did in the Old Testament strongly implies that these two witnesses may be Moses and Elijah. If so, then that is how God will fulfill His Malachi 4:5 promise: "Behold, I will send you Elijah the prophet before the coming of the great and dreadful day of the LORD."

A SIGNIFICANT ADDENDUM

Why will God cause the dark cosmic disturbances of the sun, moon, and stars in conjunction with His Day of the Lord judgments?

Early in Israel's history, Moses solemnly warned the Israelites, "And take heed, lest you lift your eyes to heaven, and when you see the sun, the moon, and the stars, all the host of heaven, you feel driven to worship them and serve them, which the LORD your God has given to all the peoples under the whole heaven as a heritage" (Dt. 4:19).

God demanded the following:

> *If there is found among you [anyone], . . . who has gone and served other gods and worshiped them, either the sun or moon or any of the host of heaven, which I have not commanded, and it is told you, and you hear of it, then you shall inquire diligently. And if it is indeed true and certain that such an abomination has been committed in Israel, then you shall bring out to your gates that man or woman who has committed that wicked thing, and shall stone to death that man or woman with stones* (17:2–5).

Evil kings of Judah had ordained idolatrous priests "to burn incense . . . to Baal, to the sun, to the moon, to the constellations, and to all the host of heaven" (2 Ki. 23:5). King Manasseh "built altars for all the host of heaven in the two courts of the house of the LORD" (21:5) and "worshiped all the host of heaven and served them" (2 Chr. 33:3).

Shortly after Manasseh's death, Josiah, a godly man, became king over Judah. He overthrew the worship of the sun, moon, and stars and restored the worship required by God:

Nevertheless the LORD did not turn from the fierceness of His great wrath, with which His anger was aroused against Judah, because of all the provocations with which Manasseh had provoked Him. And the LORD said, "I will also remove Judah from My sight, as I have removed Israel, and will cast off this city Jerusalem which I have chosen, and the house of which I said, 'My name shall be there'" (2 Ki. 23:26–27).

God was preparing Babylon to be His instrument of judgment on the kingdom of Judah.

God also appointed Jeremiah as His prophet to Judah during the reign of godly King Josiah (Jer. 1:1–2). Josiah was killed in battle against the king of Egypt (2 Ki. 23:28–30). As a result, Egypt dominated Judah until King Nebuchadnezzar of Babylon rose to power and took control (24:1–7).

God told Jeremiah to warn Judah of the desolation the Babylonians would bring on them and their cities, including Jerusalem, because the Israelites worshiped false gods and the sun, moon, and stars.

Even Judah's leaders, who led the people in this false worship and later died, would not escape a form of desolation:

"At that time," says the LORD, "they shall bring out the bones of the kings of Judah, and the bones of its princes, and the bones of the priests, and the bones of the prophets, and the bones of the inhabitants of Jerusalem, out of their graves. They shall spread them before the sun and the moon and all the host of heaven, which they have loved and which they have served and after which they have walked, which they have sought and which they have worshiped. They shall not be gathered nor buried; they shall be like refuse on the face of the earth" (Jer. 8:1–2).

God caused the sun, moon, and stars to darken at the same time that He began to pour out His wrath on the people of Israel as an indication that they were being judged because they worshiped celestial bodies instead of Him.

CHAPTER 6

The Second Event: The Shaking of the Powers of the Heavens

Matthew 24:29

Following the great cosmic disturbances that no doubt will terrify Earth's inhabitants, "the powers of the heavens will be shaken" (Mt. 24:29). Jesus presented a chronological order of events, and this second major event will occur immediately after the Great Tribulation and prior to His return. It is a result of the first event.

IDENTIFICATION OF THE POWERS

The word translated "powers" most likely refers to evil spirit-beings (demons) who follow Satan in his revolt against God.[1]

God created holy angels to serve Him in His universal Kingdom. It appears He created them with different degrees of power, as evidenced by the use of varying biblical terms, such as *cherubim* (Ezek. 10:5, 18–19), *seraphim* (Isa. 6:2, 6), *archangel* (1 Th. 4:16), *prince* (Dan. 10:21), and others.

Based on these differences, God organized the angels by rank, similar to armies. God is called "LORD of hosts" numerous times in the Old Testament. The Hebrew word translated "hosts" means "armies"[2]; thus God is "LORD of armies."

The cherubim seem to constitute the highest rank of angels. Of all the angels, they seem to have the closest relationship to God, and the Bible refers to them more frequently than to any other rank of angels.

After God completed His work of creation, He looked at "everything that He had made," and His evaluation was that "indeed it was very good" (Gen. 1:31). But it did not remain that way.

God chose a magnificent cherub to hover over His presence and throne. The prophet Ezekiel described this angel as "the anointed cherub who covers" and the "covering cherub" (Ezek. 28:14, 16).

This cherub, of course, later became known as Satan, God's adversary.[3] Satan's magnificent nature and exalted position generated an evil, deep-seated pride within him that led to his rebellion against God and his determination to usurp God's position and throne. So God cast him out of heaven to a lower location (Isa. 14:12; Ezek. 28:12–17). And this fallen cherub has been battling God ever since.

In his resolve to be like God, he wanted dominion over hosts of angels. But since he was merely a creature and not the Creator, he lacked the ability to create other angels. The most he could hope for was to persuade God's angels to rebel with him.

Satan convinced a significant number to join him, as evidenced by the biblical reference to Satan and "his angels" (Rev. 12:7–9; Mt. 25:41). Those who rebelled sealed themselves into evil forever, and those who remained loyal to God confirmed themselves into sinlessness forever. The latter are called "holy angels" (Rev. 14:10; cf. Acts 10:22) and "elect angels" (1 Tim. 5:21).

The evil angels obey Satan as "the prince of the power of the air" (Eph. 2:2). The word translated "prince" means "ruler," indicating Satan is "the chief of these personified powers . . . of the air."[4] The powers are subject to him.[5]

Language scholar Werner Foerster claims that in Ephesians 2:2, Paul referred to "the idea of an organized kingdom under the single ruler Satan."[6] Another language scholar declared, "Satan is the chief of a hostile kingdom, an absolute principle of evil."[7] Thus Jesus referred to "the devil and his angels" (Mt. 25:41).

In the Greek text, Paul described these demons as "the principalities," "the powers," "the rulers of the darkness of this age," and "the spiritual hosts of wickedness in the heavenly places" (Eph. 6:12). These designations refer to "the forces of the devil with which believers have to contend. These forces are called rulers of the world in order to bring out the terrifying power of their influence and comprehensiveness of their plans, and thus to emphasize the seriousness of the situation."[8]

Paul's use of the definite article *the* before each of these designations may indicate "different spheres of influence are allotted to them, probably by their overlord (Eph. 2:2), according to the different spheres of life."[9]

SPHERES OF INFLUENCE

Two of Satan's greatest spheres of influence are religion and sex.[10] He and his demons have been waging war with God in these vital areas since the fall of man.

RELIGIOUS SPHERE

Sacrifice or service to anyone other than the God of Scripture actually constitutes worship of Satan and his demons. As Paul wrote to the Corinthian Christians,

> *The things which the Gentiles sacrifice they sacrifice to demons and not to God, and I do not want you to have fellowship with demons. You cannot drink the cup of the Lord and the cup of demons; you cannot partake of the Lord's table and of the table of demons* (1 Cor. 10:20–21).

It was "the common belief of antiquity . . . that those who partake of the cultic meal become companions of the god."[11]

SEXUAL SPHERE

Having sex with pagan temple prostitutes was a form of worship in some religions. For example, in ancient Babylonia, around 3500 to 1750 BC, temple priestesses "were looked upon as wives and concubines of the god, and in some degree all were sacred prostitutes. This practice was observed in the form of religion in the precincts of all temples."[12] Many believed sex with a "sacred" prostitute formed a union with the god to whom she was dedicated.

SPIRITUAL WARFARE

In Ephesians 6:11–12, Paul used military terminology to warn Christians they are involved in a spiritual war with Satan and his evil angels, not merely a physical war with humans. Christians' ultimate enemies are spirit-beings who want to blind them to ultimate reality, prompt them to pursue ungodly lifestyles, and deceive them into believing false worldviews.

Paul underscored that Christians, by themselves, are no match for powerful, demonic, spirit-beings. He exhorted believers, "Keep on being empowered by your position in Christ and His demonstration of the supremacy of His strength over Satan and demons that He presented during His first coming" (Eph. 6:10).[13]

Paul also instructed Christians to do the following:

Put on the whole armor of God, that you may be able to stand against the wiles of the devil. For we do not wrestle against flesh and blood, but against principalities, against powers, against the rulers of the darkness of this age, against spiritual hosts of wickedness in the heavenly places (vv. 11–12).

The word translated "wiles" refers to the deceitful, crafty methods Satan uses.[14] His strategies involve "skillful management in getting the better of an adversary or attaining an end."[15]

God's armor for Christians includes truth, righteousness, the gospel of peace, faith, the fact of salvation, God's Word, prayer, and petition for all believers (vv. 13–18).

Satan and his evil angels do not attack Christians only. The book of Daniel reveals an ongoing war between evil and holy angels over the affairs of nations. In Daniel's day, Satan assigned evil angels to Persia (Iran) and Greece to influence their policies toward Israel. God assigned Michael, a holy archangel, to Israel to defend it against attacks from Satan and his angels (Dan. 10—11).

THE SHAKING OF THE POWERS

In His Olivet Discourse, Jesus indicated that, immediately after the Great Tribulation, "the powers of the heavens will be shaken" (Mt. 24:29).

THE NATURE OF THE SHAKING

To "shake" means "to tremble with emotion," "to quiver," "to become unsteady," "to unsettle," or "to agitate or disturb profoundly in feeling."[16] The use of the passive voice[17] in the phrase *the powers of the heavens will be shaken* means the subject—the powers of the heavens—will be *receiving* the action.[18]

The evil angels do not cause the shaking. Something else that will take place immediately after the Great Tribulation will be the cause. The only other event Jesus indicated would take place during that time is the great cosmic disturbances: the sun being darkened, the moon not giving its light, and the stars falling from heaven.

THE CAUSE OF THE SHAKING

The cosmic disturbances will cause the evil angels to tremble and become unsteady or profoundly agitated because they will remember that the same type of cosmic disturbances took place in Old Testament times and that they are related to the Day of the Lord (see chapter 5). Thus they will know their judgment is near.

Because God owns and rules the heavenly and earthly realms, the biblical expression *Day of the Lord* relates strongly to God's rule of the earth and, therefore, to His sovereign purpose for world history and specific historical events. The Day of the Lord refers to God's special intervention in world events to judge His enemies, accomplish His purpose for history, and demonstrate unequivocally who He is: the one-and-only sovereign God of the universe (Isa. 2:10–21).

The expression also refers to when God determines to intervene in world events with wrathful judgment from which no one can escape. All the past Days of the Lord began at the moment the sun, moon, and stars turned dark. There was no warning that judgment was coming.

By contrast, Joel 2:30–31 explains ahead of time that these cosmic disturbances will occur before Christ's Second Coming, after the Great Tribulation: "The sun shall be turned into darkness, and the moon into blood, before the coming of the great and awesome day of the LORD."

The passage thereby identifies Christ's Second Coming as "the great and awesome day of the LORD." The word translated "the great" indicates this Day of the Lord will surpass all other Days of the Lord,[19] and Christ's coming will cause His enemies to tremble and incite fear of God's "eschatological day of judgment."[20]

A SIGNIFICANT QUESTION

Although the evil angels, whom Christ called "the powers of the heavens" (Mt. 24:29), will be shaken when the sun grows dark, the moon's light ceases, and the stars fall from heaven immediately after the Tribulation, the Bible does not indicate they were shaken by cosmic disturbances related to previous Days of the Lord. So what is it about these disturbances that will prompt Satan's angels to shake?

When the Devil and his demons are thrust down to Earth from their heavenly realm, an enraged Satan will know "he has a short time" (Rev.12:12; 1,260 days, or three and one-half years, vv. 6, 14) before God's "great and awesome day of the Lord" (Joel 2:31) wrath will strike him.

Consequently, his demonic servants will also have that same short time before God executes His wrath on them. Their banishment to Earth is a warning that God is beginning to wage war against them.

Jesus said, "Immediately after the tribulation of those days," the cosmic disturbances related to God's great and awesome Day of the Lord wrath will appear (Mt. 24:29). Apparently, no time will elapse between the end of the 1,260 days of the Great Tribulation and the beginning of the cosmic disturbances.

Thus the Lord designed these cosmic disturbances to put Satan and his demons on notice that God's greatest and most awesome Day-of-the-Lord wrath will engulf them when the glorified Christ descends from heaven at His Second Coming. Language scholar Walter Grundmann wrote, "The return of Christ is the manifestation of the power which He has in His exaltation. It will thus mean the destruction of every hostile force and the perfect establishment of the rule of God."[21]

CHAPTER 7

The Third and Fourth Events: The Sign and the Mourning

Matthew 24:30

Following the great cosmic disturbances and the shaking of the powers of the heavens, two more powerful events will occur prior to the Messiah's return.

THE THIRD EVENT: THE APPEARING OF THE SIGN OF THE SON OF MAN

Remember, Jesus' disciples had asked Him, "What will be the sign of Your coming, and of the end of the age?" (Mt. 24:3). It was the question that had prompted Jesus to deliver the Olivet Discourse.

SIGNIFICANCE OF THE SIGN

The question implied the disciples already knew the Messiah would return and that His future coming would be preceded by a sign that would signify the end of the age.

Jesus declared, "Then the sign of the Son of Man will appear in heaven" (v. 30). The Greek word translated "appear" commonly has "the general sense" of making a hidden item "visible" or "manifest."[1] Consequently, Greek language scholar Rudolf Bultmann claims Matthew 24:30 refers to an "eschatological manifestation"[2]—a future sign that will show the world something uniquely related to Christ.

What is uniquely related to Christ? It may be His Second Coming to Earth as "the Son of Man." Every time our English-language version of the New Testament refers to Jesus as "the Son of Man," the Greek text always includes the definite article *tou* ("the") before the Greek word for "man."

Thus the Greek New Testament consistently refers to Jesus as "the Son of the Man." This fact indicates Jesus' humanity was passed down from Adam through His mother's line of descent (see Luke 3:23–38). Paul called Jesus "the last Adam" (1 Cor. 15:45).

Therefore, when Jesus said, "Then the sign of the Son of Man will appear in heaven" (Mt. 24:30), He was literally saying, "Then the sign of the Son of the Man will appear in heaven." At His Second Coming, Christ will return to Earth as the last Adam to undo the tragic damage caused by the first Adam: the loss of the theocratic Kingdom and the establishment of a "satanocracy." (See chapter 3.)

Adam's sin produced tragic consequences:

- Humanity fell from its state of sinless perfection.
- The theocratic Kingdom disappeared from Earth.
- Satan usurped the world system and has been dominating it ever since (Lk. 4:1–7; 1 Jn. 5:19).
- Women became subject to severe pain in childbirth (Gen. 3:16).
- Earth's soil decreased greatly in fertility, making it harder for people to grow the food they need in order to live (vv. 17–19).
- Humanity became subject to physical death (v. 19).
- Animals became wild.

God immediately told Satan how He would counter these disastrous consequences of the first Adam's original sin: "I will put enmity between you and the woman, and between your seed and her Seed; He shall bruise your head, and you shall bruise His heel" (v. 15).

God was promising that, during the course of world history, a manchild Redeemer would be born as a woman's offspring ("her Seed"). The promise implied a virgin birth. Centuries later, God confirmed this truth by sending the following messages through the prophet Isaiah:

Therefore the Lord Himself will give you a sign: Behold, the virgin shall conceive and bear a Son, and shall call His name Immanuel (Isa. 7:14).

For unto us a Child is born, unto us a Son is given; and the government

*will be upon His shoulder. And His name will be called Wonderful,
Counselor, Mighty God, Everlasting Father, Prince of Peace. Of the
increase of His government and peace there will be no end, upon the
throne of David and over His kingdom, to order it and establish it
with judgment and justice from that time forward, even forever. The
zeal of the LORD of hosts will perform this* (9:6–7).

In Genesis 3:15, God uses language that fit the serpent form Satan
assumed when he deceived Adam. God told Satan, "He [this man-child
Redeemer born of a woman] shall bruise [crush] your head." Just as a
human heel can crush a snake's head, so this Redeemer will crush Satan
and end his rule over the world system.

But God also told Satan, "You shall bruise His heel" (v. 15). Under
normal circumstances, if a poisonous serpent sinks its fangs into a person's bare heel, that person will die. Thus God indicated the man-child
Redeemer would die as a result of Satan's work in the world.

While Jesus and His apostles were preaching the gospel of the
Kingdom to the people of Israel, Satan followed behind, snatching
the message from individual hearts before it could take root. That fact
played a key role in those people rejecting Jesus as their Messiah and
crying out for His crucifixion (Mt. 13:19).

Matthew 1:18–25 clearly indicates Jesus Christ is the man-child
Redeemer born of a woman:

*Now the birth of Jesus Christ was as follows: After His mother Mary
was betrothed to Joseph, before they came together, she was found with
child of the Holy Spirit. Then Joseph her husband, being a just man,
and not wanting to make her a public example, was minded to put
her away secretly. But while he thought about these things, behold,
an angel of the Lord appeared to him in a dream, saying, "Joseph, son
of David, do not be afraid to take to you Mary your wife, for that
which is conceived in her is of the Holy Spirit. And she will bring
forth a Son, and you shall call His name JESUS, for He will save His
people from their sins." So all this was done that it might be fulfilled
which was spoken by the Lord through the prophet, saying: "Behold,
the virgin shall be with child, and bear a Son, and they shall call His
name Immanuel," which is translated, "God with us." Then Joseph,*

being aroused from sleep, did as the angel of the Lord commanded him
and took to him his wife, and did not know her till she had brought
forth her firstborn Son. And he called His name JESUS.

The eternal, sinless, divine Son of God took upon Himself sinless
humanity as a result of a virgin birth through a female descendant of
the first Adam. This fact implies the sin nature is passed on through
the male, not the female. Thus Jesus became qualified as the last Adam,
the One who could reverse the tragic damage the first Adam caused.

As the last Adam, Jesus could do the following:
- Crush Satan's usurped rule of the world system.
- Imprison Satan in the bottomless pit.
- Restore God's theocratic-Kingdom rule to Earth.
- Restore the original fertility of Earth's soil.
- Restore great longevity of life.
- Tame all animals.

Consequently, Jesus told His apostles, "Assuredly I say to you, that in
the regeneration, when the Son of Man sits on the throne of His glory,
you who have followed Me will also sit on twelve thrones, judging the
twelve tribes of Israel" (19:28). The Greek words translated "regeneration"
literally mean "genesis" or "beginning again." Jesus was saying that, when
He, as the last Adam, restores God's theocratic-Kingdom rule to the
earth in the future Millennium, nature will experience a new beginning.

IDENTIFICATION OF THE SIGN

Jesus did not describe the sign of the Son of the Man that will appear
after the great cosmic disturbances and the shaking of the powers of the
heavens. Consequently, no one really knows what this sign will be. The
fact that it will appear in heaven indicates it will be visible to everyone
on Earth and will significantly impact all humanity.

Biblically, signs have played key roles in relation to ancient events
and are associated with significant acts of God in world history. The
Old Testament records numerous examples, many of which were the
plagues God brought on the Egyptians when He intended to release
the Israelites from their bondage in Egypt.

Old Testament language scholar F. J. Helfmeyer wrote, "The significant thing about a sign is not the sign itself, but its function. Therefore,

a sign has an auxiliary function, since it calls attention to, confirms, or corroborates something beyond itself."[3] Thus, he wrote, "The signs which God worked in Egypt were not designed primarily to terrify Pharaoh and his people, but to cause him to acknowledge 'that I am Yahweh' (Ex. 7:3, cf. v.5)."[4]

The miracles Jesus performed during His First Coming were signs to demonstrate He was (and is) the promised Messiah, the last Adam, who will restore God's theocratic Kingdom to Earth. He calmed a fierce storm on the Sea of Galilee; walked on water; healed the deaf, the blind, the lame, and people with other illnesses; cast out demons; raised the dead to life; instantly tamed a wild donkey that had never been sat upon; multiplied a small lunch into enough food to feed a huge crowd; and caused a multitude of fish to appear while His disciples were fishing.

These miraculous signs persuaded people He was the promised Messiah: "And many of the people believed in Him, and said, 'When the Christ comes, will He do more signs than these which this Man has done?'" (Jn. 7:31).

But significant scribes and Pharisees—religious leaders of Israel—and various others claimed Jesus cast out demons using the power of Satan, the ruler of the demons (Mt. 9:34; 12:24; Lk. 11:15). They challenged Jesus to show them a visible sign from heaven so they could see it and believe in Him (Mt. 12:38; 16:1; Lk. 11:16; Jn. 6:30). Greek language scholar Karl Heinrich Rengstorf claims, "The point of the demand is that Jesus should undertake to show thereby that God, in whose name He works, has unequivocally authorized Him."[5]

But Jesus answered them,

An evil and adulterous generation seeks after a sign, and no sign will be given to it except the sign of the prophet Jonah. For as Jonah was three days and three nights in the belly of the great fish, so will the Son of [the] Man be three days and three nights in the heart of the earth. The men of Nineveh will rise up in the judgment with this generation and condemn it, because they repented at the preaching of Jonah; and indeed a greater than Jonah is here (Mt. 12:39–41).

Jesus' response may provide a clue concerning the identification of the sign of the Son of the Man. It cannot be the unmistakable coming of Christ out of heaven because Matthew 24:30 indicates Christ will not return visibly until later. The sign will appear after the cosmic disturbances and the shaking of the powers of the heavens.

It seems to me that the sign may be a portrayal of Jesus emerging alive from the empty tomb after three days and three nights, just as Jonah emerged alive after three days and three nights in the belly of a great fish. I believe such a sign would demonstrate that Satan, who worked diligently to have Jesus rejected and killed, still failed to thwart Him from returning to restore and administer God's theocratic-Kingdom rule over Earth for its last 1,000 years (13:19; Jn. 12:31; 14:30; Acts 3:14–15; 2 Cor. 4:4; Eph. 2:1–2; 1 Jn. 5:19).

After Jesus was buried, the chief priests and Pharisees persuaded Pontius Pilate, the Roman prefect, to make Christ's tomb totally secure for three days to prevent His disciples from stealing His body and saying, "He has risen from the dead" (Mt. 27:62–66). Perhaps that was Satan's way of trying to prevent Jesus' resurrection so He could not perform His duty as the last Adam.

I believe the sign of Jesus walking out of the empty tomb alive after three days and three nights—with the wounds of His crucifixion in His hands, feet, and side (Lk. 24:39–49; Jn. 20:25–26)—would powerfully affect the entire planet's population and communicate that Earth was about to experience major changes. It would demonstrate that the last Adam—who was crucified for the sins of the world, was about to return to end Satan's rule, restore God's theocratic Kingdom, and remove a destructive curse from nature.

THE FOURTH EVENT: ALL THE TRIBES OF THE EARTH WILL MOURN

Whatever the sign turns out to be, when it appears in heaven it will have a profound impact on humanity. Jesus said, "All the tribes of the earth will mourn" (Mt. 24:30).

ISRAELITE MOURNING

Since the words translated "the earth" can also mean "the land," some interpreters believe this is a reference exclusively to the mourning of all the tribes of Israel. Zechariah 12:10–12 foretold such Israelite mourning:

And I will pour on the house of David and on the inhabitants of

Jerusalem the Spirit of grace and supplication; then they will look on Me whom they pierced. Yes, they will mourn for Him as one mourns for his only son, and grieve for Him as one grieves for a firstborn. In that day there shall be a great mourning in Jerusalem, like the mourning at Hadad Rimmon in the plain of Megiddo. And the land shall mourn, every family by itself.

When Jerusalem and the nation of Israel are desperate, surrounded by the armies of all the other nations, all the families in Jerusalem will mourn for the One who was pierced by crucifixion. It may be that the sign of the Son of the Man in heaven opens their eyes to the reality that Jesus is, indeed, Israel's true Messiah.

Unfortunately, Israel has been blind to that reality. Over the centuries, the nation's religious leaders have emphasized the Mosaic Law and Jewish tradition over the divinely inspired Messianic prophecies. To this day, most Jewish people do not know that more than 700 years before Jesus was born, God revealed to them through the Jewish prophet Isaiah that the Messiah would be born of a virgin (Isa. 7:14) and shoulder the responsibility of governing God's worldwide Kingdom (9:6–7).

Most Jewish people also are unaware of Isaiah 53, which foretold that, when the Messiah would be on Earth, few in Israel would believe the report that the future Kingdom of God was at hand:

Who has believed our report? And to whom has the arm of the LORD been revealed? He is despised and rejected by men, a Man of sorrows and acquainted with grief. And we hid, as it were, our faces from Him; He was despised, and we did not esteem Him. Surely He has borne our griefs and carried our sorrows; yet we esteemed Him stricken, smitten by God, and afflicted. But He was wounded for our transgressions, He was bruised for our iniquities; the chastisement for our peace was upon Him, and by His stripes we are healed (vv. 1, 3–5).

Despite the fact that Jesus revealed "the arm of the LORD" (the miraculous powers necessary to establish the Kingdom of God), He would be despised and rejected by Israel and die as a sacrificial Lamb for the sins of mankind.

And, of course, another reason for Israel's blindness today revolves around the cruel way organized Christendom has treated the Jewish people for more than 2,000 years.

INTERNATIONAL MOURNING

The word translated "tribes" in the context of Matthew 24:30 can also mean "nations, people."[6] This meaning would imply that the people of all nations will mourn when they see the sign of the Son of the Man in heaven.

Their mourning, however, will have a vastly different significance than Israel's mourning. Since most, if not all, other nations will never have seen such a heavenly sign, it will have ominous, threatening implications, prompting them to mourn.

Rengstorf said, "From the context [of Matthew 24:30], one may gather only that it is something which is clearly terrifying, since it causes all races on earth to strike up a lament for themselves in their last hopeless distress."[7]

Similarly, New Testament language scholar Gustav Stahlin wrote that the mourning of the Gentile nations will constitute "grief at one's personal fate, at the immediately impending judgment of God, concerning which the sign manifested in heaven precludes all further doubt. Eschatological mourning is mourning in the most specific and eternally valid sense. It is the world's mourning for itself in its final hopeless distress."[8]

CHAPTER 8

The Second Coming of Jesus Christ

Matthew 24:30

Now we come to the grand event, the phenomenon that will shatter Satan's power, transform the Earth, and change life on this planet forever: the Second Coming of the Lord Jesus Christ. It is specifically mentioned in two New Testament passages: Matthew 24:30 and Revelation 1:7.

Matthew 24:30 says that, after the sign of the Son of the Man appears and causes all the tribes of the earth to mourn, "they will see the Son of Man coming on the clouds of heaven with power and great glory."

Revelation 1:7 declares, "Behold, He is coming with clouds, and every eye will see Him, even they who pierced Him. And all the tribes of the earth will mourn because of Him. Even so, Amen."

CHRIST'S PAROUSIA

Over the centuries, the Greek word *parousia* has been applied to Christ's Second Coming. At first, in the general, secular realm, it meant "presence, coming, advent as the first stage in presence." In the special, technical sense, it meant "the coming of a hidden divinity, who makes his presence felt by a revelation of his power, or whose presence is celebrated in the cult." *Parousia* also became "the official term for a visit of a person of high rank, especially of kings and emperors visiting a province."[1]

When applied to Christ, it almost always refers to "His Messianic advent in glory to judge the world at the end of this age."[2] Greek language scholar Albrecht Oepke wrote that the "parousia" of Christ is "the *parousia*, in which history is anchored," and "the point where history is mastered by God's eternal rule."[3]

The Greek text of Matthew 24:30 literally states that Christ returns to Earth as "the Son of the Man" (Adam). He will end Satan's rule over the world system, have Satan bound and imprisoned in what is called "the bottomless pit" for 1,000 years (Rev. 20:3), and restore God's theocratic-Kingdom rule to Earth for the last millennium of this earth's history (vv. 4–6). After that time, Satan will be "cast into the lake of fire and brimstone where the beast and the false prophet are. And they will be tormented day and night forever and ever" (v. 10).

And so will end Satan's age-old battle with God and his prideful, arrogant, and useless quest to be like the Most High.

CLOUDS OF HEAVEN

For millennia, one of Satan's most effective tactics to prevent people from being delivered "from the power of darkness and conveyed . . . into the kingdom of the Son of His love" (1 Cor. 1:13) has been to convince them Jesus is not God. The deity of Christ is one of the biggest stumbling blocks many people face in coming to faith in Jesus as Messiah. Jewish people, Mormons, Christian Scientists, Muslims, Buddhists, Hindus, Scientologists, and an amazingly long list of others also do not believe Jesus is God.

It is not without design, therefore, that Jesus told His disciples in the Olivet Discourse that He will return "on the clouds of heaven" (Mt. 24:30). Remember, the New Testament had not been written. His disciples had only the Hebrew Scriptures, and passages there distinctly indicate that clouds are God's vehicle for movement, at least for God the Father:

- Psalm 104:3—"[God] makes the clouds His chariot."
- Isaiah 19:1—"The LORD rides on a swift cloud."
- Nahum 1:3—"The clouds are the dust of His feet."

But a significant Old Testament passage indicates that clouds will also be the vehicle for another person, one whom the prophet Daniel saw in a dream several centuries before Jesus was born as the Son of the Man.

DANIEL'S VISION

Daniel wrote, "I was watching in the night visions, and behold, One like the Son of Man, coming with the clouds of heaven! He came to the Ancient of Days, and they brought Him near before Him" (Dan. 7:13–14).

The expression "the Son of Man" indicates this person was human. But the word *like* implies He was more than human. Since this Son of Man was coming "with the clouds of heaven," the logical conclusion is that Daniel saw someone who was God incarnate.

Ancient Jewish writers believed he was the Messiah.[4] Jesus implied the same, for He claimed to be the Son of the Man who would come with the clouds of heaven (Mt. 24:30; 26:64). The apostle John also recognized Jesus as this individual (Rev. 1:7; 14:14).

In Daniel's dream, the Son of Man "came to the Ancient of Days, and they brought Him near before Him" (Dan. 7:13). Clearly, the language implies the Messiah and Ancient of Days are two distinct persons. The Ancient of Days is God the Father.

The Messiah, or Son of Man, was then "given dominion and glory and a kingdom, that all peoples, nations, and languages should serve Him. His dominion is an everlasting dominion, which shall not pass away, and His kingdom the one which shall not be destroyed" (v. 14).

Commenting on the language of Daniel 7:13–14, Oepke wrote, "The one like unto the Son of Man . . . is a visionary embodiment of theocracy in distinction from worldly powers, he comes with the clouds of heaven. He receives all power from the Ancient of days (God)."[5] Oepke indicated Daniel's vision foretold that when Christ comes as the Son of Man on the clouds of heaven at His Second Coming, He will come with God's full authority to end Satan's rule over the world system and restore to Earth God's theocratic Kingdom.

He will be Israel's divine King-Messiah who "sits on the throne of His glory" (Mt. 19:28)—God's final representative to administer His rule over the entire earth and bring blessing to the entire world (25:31–34; Acts 3:19–21; 1 Cor. 15:23–25, 45; Rev. 20:4–6).

CHRIST'S ADMISSION

When Jesus was brought before the chief priests, the elders, and all of Israel's council, they tried to obtain false testimony against Him to justify executing Him. Finally, two false witnesses accused Him of claiming He could destroy God's Temple and build it in three days (Mt. 26:59–61).

The high priest challenged Jesus to respond to these accusations, but Jesus kept silent. Then the high priest said to Him, "I put You under oath by the living God: Tell us if You are the Christ, the Son of God!" (v. 63).

Jesus responded, "It is as you said. Nevertheless, I say to you, hereafter you will see the Son of Man sitting at the right hand of the Power, and coming on the clouds of heaven" (v. 64).

The high priest tore his clothes and told the rest of the council, "He has spoken blasphemy! What further need do we have of witnesses? Look, now you have heard His blasphemy! What do you think?" (vv. 65–66).

Their answer, "He is deserving of death" (v. 66), shows they recognized He was claiming to be deity because they believed only God comes on the clouds of heaven.

Jesus's statement to His disciples that, He will return on the clouds was confirmed to them on the day of His ascension:

> *While they watched, He was taken up, and a cloud received Him out of their sight. And while they looked steadfastly toward heaven as He went up, behold, two men stood by them in white apparel, who also said, "Men of Galilee, why do you stand gazing up into heaven? This same Jesus, who was taken up from you into heaven, will so come in like manner as you saw Him go into heaven"* (Acts 1:9–11).

CHRIST'S POWER

Jesus also told His disciples He will come "with power" (Mt. 24:30). The word translated "power" refers to "might, strength, force."[6] Grundmann indicated it refers to "the one who can do something," and it historically referred to one "who exercises authority and rule."[7]

Grundmann pointed out, "In place of the neutral forces of nature we have the power and might of the personal God."[8] In contrast with the gods of pagan nations, which were "essentially nature gods," the "God of the OT is the God of history."[9]

In Jeremiah 27:5, God declared, "I have made the earth, the man and the beast that are on the ground, by My great power and by My outstretched arm, and have given it to whom it seemed proper to Me. "

Jeremiah declared, "You are great in counsel and mighty in work, for Your eyes are open to all the ways of the sons of men, to give everyone according to his ways and according to the fruit of his doings" (32:19).

The fact that God has the authoritative power to create and control what will transpire over time indicates He ultimately determines what will happen to the universe, the heavens, the earth, nations, mankind, animals, Satan, fallen and holy angels, vegetation, and climate conditions. He has the authority to crush Satan and his rule of the world system through Christ's Second Coming.

Grundmann explained, "The eschatological exercise of God's power is basically an overthrow of demonic powers. Between God and humanity there interpose themselves forces which partly fight against God and partly for Him, i.e., the forces of angels and demons."[10] Demons fight against God, and the holy angels fight for Him.

Grundmann also accurately recognized that, during His First Coming, Jesus' miracles of overcoming "the kingdom of demonic powers ruling in sickness, sin and death" were samples of "the dominion of God overcoming and expelling the sway of demons and Satan."[11]

When the Pharisees heard Jesus healed demon-possessed people of their blindness and inability to speak, they said, "This fellow does not cast out demons except by Beelzebub, the ruler of the demons" (Mt. 12:24). They apparently believed this feat was only possible through Satan's approval and empowerment. Jesus knew their thoughts and responded to their erroneous conclusion:

> *Every kingdom divided against itself is brought to desolation, and every city or house divided against itself will not stand. If Satan casts out Satan, he is divided against himself. How then will his kingdom stand? And if I cast out demons by Beelzebub, by whom do your sons cast them out? Therefore they shall be your judges. But if I cast out demons by the Spirit of God, surely the kingdom of God has come upon you. Or how can one enter a strong man's house and plunder his goods, unless he first binds the strong man? And then he will plunder his house* (vv. 25–29).

Jesus' response indicated that His miracles showed the superiority of the powers of the Kingdom of God over the kingdom of Satan: "If I cast out demons by the Spirit of God, surely the kingdom of God has come upon you" (v. 28). His miracles were previews of the supreme powers Christ will fully exercise at His Second Coming, when He completely eradicates Satan's powers and restores God's theocratic-Kingdom rule to Earth for its last 1,000 years.

Thus, when Jesus spoke of His "coming on the clouds of heaven with power" (24:30), He was referring to "the manifestation of the power which He has in His exaltation. It will thus mean the destruction of every hostile force and the perfect establishment of the rule of God."[12]

CHRIST'S GLORY

Jesus also indicated that at His Second Advent, all the world will see Him come with "great glory" (v. 30). The Greek word *doxa*, translated "glory," literally means "brightness, splendor, radiance" and, when describing Christ, refers to "majestic power."[13] In the New Testament, *doxa* communicates "the senses of 'reputation' and 'power' . . . [and] is also used strictly in the New Testament to express the 'divine mode of being.'"[14]

The word translated "great" means "much, great, strong, profound."[15] It indicates that at Christ's Second Coming, He will descend from heaven with such strong and profound brightness, splendor, and radiance that His majestic power and deity will be unmistakable. Together with the sign of the Son of the Man, this unparalleled display of majesty will reveal to the world that Jesus is returning as a *theanthropic* (divine-human) person.[16]

CHRIST'S TRIUMPH

The Jewish prophet Daniel's vision (Dan. 7:13–27) several centuries before Jesus' birth unveils important details concerning Christ's Second Coming. Although we've noted some of these details earlier, they are so significant they warrant repeating.

In the future, a global kingdom will dominate the entire world. After a time, a new ruler will rise to power within this kingdom. He will blaspheme God, persecute for three and one-half years those who worship God, and try to change times and law (vv. 23–25).

He will do so until the "Ancient of Days" (God) comes (v. 22), and the "court" of heaven determines to "take away his dominion [kingdom], to consume and destroy it forever" (v. 26). Then a great and long-anticipated moment will arrive: "And a judgment was made in favor of the saints of the Most High, and the time came for the saints to possess the kingdom" (v. 22). The Antichrist's satanically driven kingdom and power will be on the verge of being smashed forever by the returning Lord Jesus Christ:

> *One like the Son of Man, coming with the clouds of heaven . . . came to the Ancient of Days . . . Then to Him was given dominion and glory and a kingdom, that all peoples, nations, and languages should serve Him. His dominion is an everlasting dominion, which shall not pass away, and His kingdom the one which shall not be destroyed. [And] the saints of the Most High shall receive the kingdom, and possess the kingdom forever, even forever and ever* (vv. 13–14, 18).

As the book of Daniel teaches, the Messiah will restore God's theocratic Kingdom to Earth. New Testament language scholar Helmut Traub stated that the Bible describes heaven as "the upper and controlling part of the universe, which is always described as heaven and earth." Traub emphasized that, although heaven and Earth are part of the same universe, the Bible indicates they are separate entities. Heaven is God's home; Earth is not.

Because God created the earth, He rightfully has the lordship authority to deal with it as He sees fit.[17] Thus He has the authority to send His Son, Jesus the Messiah, from heaven as the Son of the Man, the last Adam, to end Satan's rule over the world system and restore His theocratic-Kingdom rule to Earth.

CHAPTER 9

The Gathering of the Elect

Matthew 24:31

In conjunction with His Second Coming to Earth, Jesus "will send His angels with a great sound of a trumpet, and they will gather together His elect from the four winds, from one end of heaven to the other" (Mt. 24:31).

Greek language scholar Karl Heinrich Rengstorf claimed the verb translated "will send" refers to a commission that requires the person who is sent to speak and act exactly how the sender would speak and act.[1] "In other words," he said, "the emphasis rests on the fact of sending in conjunction with the one who sends, not on the one who is sent."[2] Those sent represent their sender and his authority.[3]

So in concurrence with His Second Coming, Jesus will commission His holy angels to represent Him by accomplishing what He Himself wants done—the gathering of His elect people from all over the world.

IDENTIFICATION OF CHRIST'S ELECT

Who are the elect whom the holy angels will gather at Christ's Second Coming after the Great Tribulation? Some sincere Christians believe they are church saints. They believe in Matthew 24 Christ was referring to the Rapture of the church in conjunction with His Second Coming. If that view were correct, the church would have to endure all or part of the Great Tribulation before being removed from the earth.

However, several factors indicate the gathering of the elect in Matthew 24:31 refers not to the Rapture but to the gathering of the remnant of Israel alive on Earth when Jesus returns:

First, the term *elect* in the Bible is not used exclusively for church saints. Many times God uses it to refer to Israel. Second, no biblical evidence indicates the church has replaced Israel in God's plan. Israel remains God's elect nation. Third, Jesus' description of the gathering of the elect "from the four winds, from one end of heaven to the other" (v. 31) echoes Old Testament prophecies of God gathering the nation of Israel.

ISRAEL AS GOD'S ELECT

Many passages teach unequivocally that God made national Israel His elect, or chosen, people in contrast with all other nations. The Jewish people occupy a special place in His economy:

Deuteronomy 7:6. Moses told the people of Israel, "You are a holy people to the LORD your God; the LORD your God has chosen you to be a people for Himself, a special treasure above all the peoples on the face of the earth." The word translated "holy" means "set apart, consecrated."[4]

Commenting on this and other similar statements in Deuteronomy, language scholar G. Quell wrote that Deuteronomy "established the concept of election in the sense of the designation of Israel as the people of God."[5] With regard to election, "The nations," he wrote, "did not experience what Israel experienced."[6]

1 Chronicles 16:13. "O seed of Israel His [the Lord's] servant, you children of Jacob, His chosen ones!"

Isaiah 45:4. God called the nation "Israel My elect."

Romans 11:28–29. The apostle Paul told the church saints in Rome, "Concerning the gospel they [the Jewish people] are enemies for your sake, but concerning the election they are beloved for the sake of the fathers. For the gifts and the calling of God are irrevocable."

New Testament language scholar Gottlob Schrenk pointed out Paul used "the term for the election of all Israel in the fathers. Here the reference is not to a part but to the whole people."[7]

Paul thereby indicated that, although Israel had disobeyed and rebelled against God numerous times, Israel was still His beloved, elect nation.

ISRAEL REMAINS GOD'S ELECT NATION

Because of the irrevocable covenant God established with Israel's ancestors—Abraham, Isaac, and Jacob—Israel remains God's elect nation.
He has neither abandoned them nor permanently cast them off. The
following passages affirm this covenant:

Genesis 12:1–3. "Now the LORD had said to Abram: 'Get out of your
country, from your family and from your father's house, to a land that
I will show you. I will make you a great nation; I will bless you and
make your name great; and you shall be a blessing. I will bless those
who bless you, and I will curse him who curses you; and in you all the
families of the earth shall be blessed.'"

Genesis 12:7. "Then the LORD appeared to Abram and said, 'To your
descendants I will give this land.'"

Genesis 13:14–15. "And the LORD said to Abram, after Lot had
separated from him: 'Lift your eyes now and look from the place where
you are—northward, southward, eastward, and westward; for all the
land which you see I give to you and your descendants forever.'" (Note
the word *forever.*)

Genesis 15:13–14, 18. "On the same day the LORD made a covenant
with Abram, saying: 'To your descendants I have given this land, from
the river of Egypt to the great river, the River Euphrates'" (v. 18).

On that same day, God also clearly defined what He meant by
Abram's "descendants": "Know certainly that your descendants will be
strangers in a land that is not theirs, and will serve them, and they will
afflict them four hundred years. And also the nation whom they serve
I will judge; afterward they shall come out with great possessions" (vv.
13–14).

God obviously was referring to Israel's enslavement in Egypt for
400 years. He later delivered them out of Egypt, and they escaped with
great wealth from the Egyptians. (See the book of Exodus.)

Genesis 17:5, 7–8. God changed Abram's name to Abraham and
declared, "I will establish My covenant between Me and you and your
descendants after you in their generations, for an everlasting covenant,
to be God to you and your descendants after you. Also I give to you and
your descendants after you the land in which you are a stranger, all the
land of Canaan, as an everlasting possession; and I will be their God"
(vv. 7–8). (Note the words *everlasting covenant* and *everlasting possession.*)

ISHMAEL AND ISAAC

Although Abraham had an older son than Isaac, God did not choose him. He chose Isaac and made His choice clear.

Abraham's firstborn came into the world because Abraham's wife, Sarah, who was barren, persuaded him to father a child through her Egyptian maid Hagar. They named that son Ishmael (16:1–4, 15).

Several years later, at 90 years of age, Sarah bore a son to Abraham. God commanded them to name that son Isaac and said, "I will establish My covenant with him for an everlasting covenant, and with his descendants after him" (17:19). (Note: The everlasting covenant God established with Abraham, which involved the everlasting possession of the land of Canaan, would continue to be everlasting with Isaac and his biological descendants.)

In response to Abraham's plea for God to bless his son Ishmael (v. 18), God responded, "And as for Ishmael, I have heard you. Behold, I have blessed him, and will make him fruitful, and will multiply him exceedingly. He shall beget twelve princes, and I will make him a great nation. But My covenant I will establish with Isaac, whom Sarah shall bear to you at this set time next year" (vv. 20–21).

God clearly distinguished between these two sons and their descendants. He would bless Ishmael and his descendants, but that blessing would not include the everlasting Abrahamic Covenant, with its "everlasting possession" of the land.

That distinction is extremely significant. Historically, the Arabs have claimed they are descendants of Ishmael and the rightful owners of Israel's land. Clearly, God did not give the land to them.

MOSES' STATEMENT TO GOD

Remember Abraham, Isaac, and Israel, Your servants, to whom You swore by Your own self, and said to them, "I will multiply your descendants as the stars of heaven; and all this land that I have spoken of I give to your descendants, and they shall inherit it forever" (Ex. 32:13). (Note the word *forever*.)

KING DAVID'S STATEMENT TO GOD

And who is like Your people, like Israel, the one nation on the earth whom God went to redeem for Himself as a people, to make for Himself a name—and to do for Yourself great and awesome deeds for Your land—before Your people whom You redeemed for Yourself from Egypt, the nations, and their gods? For You have made Your people Israel Your very own people forever; and You, LORD, have become their God (2 Sam. 7:23–24). (Again, note the word *forever.*)

GOD'S STATEMENT CONCERNING ISRAEL'S REBELLION

The land also shall be left empty by them, and will enjoy its sabbaths while it lies desolate without them; they will accept their guilt, because they despised My judgments and because their soul abhorred My statutes. Yet for all that, when they are in the land of their enemies, I will not cast them away, nor shall I abhor them, to utterly destroy them and break My covenant with them; for I am the LORD their God. But for their sake I will remember the covenant of their ancestors, whom I brought out of the land of Egypt in the sight of the nations, that I might be their God: I am the LORD (Lev. 26:43–45).

GOD'S STATEMENT CONCERNING ISRAEL'S COMING CAPTIVITY IN BABYLON

"Therefore do not fear, O My servant Jacob," says the LORD, "nor be dismayed, O Israel; for behold, I will save you from afar, and your seed from the land of their captivity. Jacob shall return, have rest and be quiet, and no one shall make him afraid. For I am with you," says the LORD, "to save you; though I make a full end of all nations where I have scattered you, yet I will not make a complete end of you. But I will correct you in justice, and will not let you go altogether unpunished" (Jer. 30:10–11).

THE APOSTLE PETER'S STATEMENTS

After the church was born on Pentecost, Peter spoke in the Temple, confronting a crowd of Jewish people who had cried out for Jesus' crucifixion when He was on trial before Pilate:

Men of Israel, . . . The God of Abraham, Isaac, and Jacob, the God of our fathers, glorified His Servant Jesus, whom you delivered up and denied in the presence of Pilate, when he was determined to let Him go. But you denied the Holy One and the Just, and asked for a murderer to be granted to you, and killed the Prince of life, whom God raised from the dead, of which we are witnesses (Acts 3:12–15).

Yet despite their horrendous sin against Christ, Peter told them, "You are [note the use of the present tense "are," not past tense "were"] sons of the covenant which God made with our fathers" (v. 25). Thus, despite their terrible sin, the Abrahamic Covenant was still in effect.

THE APOSTLE PAUL'S STATEMENT

Several years after the birth of the church, Paul wrote, "I say then, has God cast away His people? Certainly not! For I also am an Israelite, of the seed of Abraham, of the tribe of Benjamin. God has not cast away His people whom He foreknew" (Rom. 11:1–2).

APOSTOLIC TEACHING

At the Last Supper, Christ told His apostles He would leave them soon to return to God the Father. Then He said to them, "The word which you hear is not Mine but the Father's who sent Me. These things I have spoken to you while being present with you. But the Helper, the Holy Spirit, whom the Father will send in My name, He will teach you all things, and bring to your remembrance all things that I said to you" (Jn. 14:24–26). Shortly thereafter He told them,

I still have many things to say to you, but you cannot bear them now. However, when He, the Spirit of truth, has come, He will guide you into all truth; for He will not speak on His own authority, but whatever He hears He will speak; and He will tell you things to come. He will glorify Me, for He will take of what is Mine and declare it to you. All things that the Father has are Mine. Therefore I said that He will take of Mine and declare it to you (16:12–15).

It is important to note to whom Jesus addressed these statements. He spoke specifically to the 12 apostles, not to all believers in general; and He indicated that, during the apostles' lifetime, the Holy Spirit would communicate to that body of men *all* (not merely some) of the truth.

Jesus did not mean the 12 were the only people to whom the Holy Spirit would reveal this truth. Although Paul was not in the corporate body of those apostles gathered with Christ, he nevertheless was an apostle, "born out of due time" (1 Cor. 15:8). The Holy Spirit also revealed truth to New Testament prophets (2:10–13; Eph. 3:3–5).

Nor did Jesus mean that each of the 12 apostles would receive *all* of this communication of knowledge from the Holy Spirit individually. Instead, the Holy Spirit would deliver this knowledge to this corporate body of men before the last apostle would die. The Holy Spirit gave John, who wrote the final book of the Bible and was the last of the 12 to die (around AD 100), significant revelation years after the other 11 apostles had passed away (Rev. 1:20; 4:1; 17:3; 21:10).

In Ephesians, Paul drew an analogy between the construction of a building and the construction of the church. He said the church was "built on the foundation of the apostles and [New Testament] prophets, Jesus Christ Himself being the chief cornerstone" (2:20). Just as the foundation of a building is laid once for all in the early stages of construction, so the church's foundation of the apostles and New Testament prophets was laid once for all through divine truth revealed to them by the Holy Spirit. That revelation ended when John died. God's Word, the Bible, was now complete.

What relationship do these facts have to the concept of Israel being God's elect? None of the church apostles and New Testament prophets taught Replacement Theology—the teaching that, because Israel as a nation rejected Jesus Christ at His First Coming, God rejected Israel as His Chosen People and replaced the nation with the church. Nowhere does the Bible teach that concept.

Church history reveals that Replacement Theology did not begin until after all the apostles and New Testament prophets had died and the Bible had been completed. In the century after John died, anti-Semitic Gentile church leaders introduced the idea that God has forever rejected Israel and replaced it with the church.

As far as God's Holy Word is concerned, the Jewish people are still the elect of God.

JESUS' DESCRIPTION OF THE GATHERING OF THE ELECT

In Matthew 24:31, Jesus said His elect will be gathered "from the four winds, from one end of heaven to the other." New Testament language scholars William F. Arndt and F. Wilbur Gingrich said the expression concerning the winds refers to "the four directions or cardinal points."[8] Jesus was claiming His elect will be gathered from all over the world at His Second Coming with His holy angels.

Four factors indicate Jesus' description of the gathering of His elect echoes the Old Testament description of the gathering of Israel.

1. Because of Israel's persistent rebellion, God promised to scatter the Jewish people "to all the winds" (Ezek. 5:10,12) and "to every wind" (17:21). In Zechariah 2:6, God said He scattered them abroad "like the four winds of heaven."

"The 'four winds,' *ruhot*," wrote theologian J. Barton Payne, "describe the four quarters or four directions of the world (Jer. 49:36; Ezek. 37:9)."[9] Thus the Old Testament reference had the same meaning as Jesus' mention of "the four winds" in Matthew 24:31. God scattered the Jewish people throughout the world.

2. God promised that, in the future, Israel will be gathered from the east, west, north, and south, "from the ends of the earth" (Isa. 43:5–7). In the context of this promise, God calls Israel His "chosen" (vv. 10, 20).

3. Jesus declared His angels will gather His elect "from one end of heaven to the other" (Mt. 24:31). Moses told the people of Israel, "If any of you are driven out to the farthest parts under heaven, from there the LORD your God will gather you, and from there He will bring you. Then the LORD your God will bring you to the land which your fathers possessed, and you shall possess it. He will prosper you and multiply you more than your fathers" (Dt. 30:4–5).

4. Jesus indicated His elect will be gathered from the four directions of the world in conjunction with the blast of "a great trumpet" (Mt. 24:31, literal Greek translation), and Isaiah 27:13 teaches the scattered children of Israel will be gathered to their homeland in conjunction with the blowing of "a great trumpet" (literal translation of the Hebrew text): "So it shall be in that day: The great trumpet will be

blown; They will come, who are about to perish in the land
of Assyria, and they who are outcasts in the land of Egypt,
and shall worship the LORD in the holy mount at Jerusalem."

Theologian Franz Delitzsch stated this teaching in Isaiah refers to
"the still living *diaspora*" being gathered together by the signal of God.[10]
He also indicated that Assyria and Egypt, referenced in this passage,
represent all the lands of exile.[11]

Theologian Gerhard Friedrich wrote that in that future eschatological
day, "a great horn shall be blown (Isa. 27:13)"; and the exiled will return
by that signal.[12] He asserted that in conjunction with the blowing of
the great trumpet, "There follows the gathering of Israel and the return
of the dispersed to Zion."[13]

It is significant to note that Isaiah 27:13, which foretells this future
regathering of Israel to its homeland, is the only specific reference in
the Old Testament to a "great" trumpet.[14]

Although Isaiah 11:10–12 does not refer to a great trumpet, it
parallels Isaiah 27:13 because it refers to the same gathering of Israel:[15]

And in that day there shall be a Root of Jesse, who shall stand as a
banner to the people; for the Gentiles shall seek Him, and His resting
place shall be glorious. It shall come to pass in that day that the Lord
shall set His hand again the second time to recover the remnant of
His people who are left, from Assyria and Egypt, from Pathros and
Cush, from Elam and Shinar, from Hamath and the islands of the
sea. He will set up a banner for the nations, and will assemble the
outcasts of Israel, and gather together the dispersed of Judah from the
four corners of the earth (11:10–12).

The word translated "banner" also means "standard," "ensign," "signal,"
and "sign."[16] Within context, Isaiah 11:10–12 indicates that when the
Messiah (Jesus Christ, a descendant of Jesse, vv. 1–9) returns to Earth
at His Second Coming as an ensign to rule and transform the world,
He will gather together the scattered remnant of His people Israel.

Commenting on the fact that Isaiah 11:11–12 and 27:13 refer to the
same gathering of Israel, theologian T. Francis Glasson wrote, "In the
O.T. and also later Jewish writings, two things are associated with the
gathering of the dispersed: the trumpet and the ensign (or standard). The

following prayer still appears in the Jewish Daily Prayer Book: 'Sound the *great trumpet* for our freedom; lift up the *ensign* to gather our exiles, and gather us from the four corners of the earth. Blessed art thou, O Lord, who gatherest the banished ones of thy people Israel.' (Quoted from *Authorized Daily Prayer Book of the United Hebrew Congregations of the British Empire* [S. Singer], p. 48)." [17]

In their New Year service, in which they pray almost identically this same prayer, Jewish people quote Isaiah 27:13 and 11:12. [18]

The Apocalypse of Abraham, an ancient piece of Jewish literature written between 200 BC and AD 200, states, "Then will I blow the trumpet from the winds and send forth mine elect ... he then summons my despised people out of all nations." [19] "Mine elect" refers to God's Messiah, who will gather together God's scattered people. [20]

CHAPTER 10

Parables Related to Christ's Second Coming

Matthew 24:32–51

After Jesus told His apostles that His holy angels will gather His elect people of Israel from all over the world in conjunction with His Second Coming, He launched into several parables and illustrations that often are misunderstood today. The first is the parable of the fig tree.

THE PARABLE OF THE FIG TREE

> *Now learn this parable from the fig tree: When its branch has already become tender and puts forth leaves, you know that summer is near. So you also, when you see all these things, know that it is near—at the doors! Assuredly, I say to you, this generation will by no means pass away till all these things take place. Heaven and earth will pass away, but My words will by no means pass away. But of that day and hour no one knows, not even the angels of heaven, but My Father only* (Mt. 24:32–36).

Some sincere Christians believe the fig tree represents Israel. They espouse that the tender branch putting forth leaves represents Israel's rebirth as a modern nation in its God-given homeland in 1948. But if this were true, that generation would not pass away before Christ's return and the end of the present pre-Messianic Age.

Some people who held this view claimed 20 years equals a generation and, therefore, Christ would return by 1968. But 1968 came and went without Christ's advent. Then some claimed 40 years equals a generation, and Christ would return by 1988. But 1988 also came and went.

The fig tree does not represent Israel and its rebirth in 1948, and here is why:

THE PARABLE'S PURPOSE WAS TO POINT TO CHRIST'S IMMINENT RETURN

The establishment of the State of Israel did not coincide with that event. New Testament language scholar Friedrich Hauck wrote, "Many of the parables of Jesus seek to clarify for the hearers the nature and coming of the kingdom of God." He said, "[Jesus] speaks in parables about the imminent establishment of God's kingdom (the fig tree, Mk. 13:28 f., Lk. 21:29–31), [and] its sudden coming (the thief, Mt. 24:43 f.; Lk.12:39 f.)."[1]

LUKE SUPPORTS THIS CONCLUSION

"Then He spoke to them a parable: 'Look at the fig tree, and all the trees. When they are already budding, you see and know for yourselves that summer is now near. So you also, when you see these things happening, know that the kingdom of God is near. Assuredly, I say to you, this generation will by no means pass away till all things take place'" (Lk. 21:29–32).

If the budding fig tree represented Israel's rebirth, then what do all the other budding trees represent?

JESUS INDICATES MORE THAN ONE EVENT IS INVOLVED

The phrase *all these things* refers to all the other developments Jesus mentioned from the beginning of His discourse: the beginning of birth pangs, persecution of believers, loss of civility and affection, lawlessness, false prophets, the worldwide preaching of the gospel of the Kingdom, the abomination of desolation in the Temple in Jerusalem, and the Great Tribulation (Mt 24:4–21). No combination of these circumstances occurred before Israel was restored to its homeland in 1948.

THE GENERATION ALIVE ON EARTH WILL NOT PASS AWAY BEFORE CHRIST'S SECOND COMING

In other words, the generation that will be alive to witness the events of the Tribulation will be the generation that sees Jesus return to Earth. To stress the certainty of His coming at that time, Jesus said, "Heaven and earth will pass away, but My words will by no means pass away" (v. 35).

Through the parable of the fig tree, Jesus indicated that the people on Earth during the Tribulation will be able to know with certainty they are in the time immediately preceding Christ's Second Coming and that their generation will not pass away before He returns. However, they still will not know the precise day or hour of His coming. Jesus said, "But of that day and hour no one knows, not even the angels of heaven, but My Father only" (v. 36).

THE PARALLEL WITH THE DAYS OF NOAH

The order of circumstances at Christ's Second Coming will parallel the order of circumstances in Noah's days: "But as the days of Noah were, so also will the coming of the Son of Man be" (v. 37).

Noah, a "preacher of righteousness" (2 Pet. 2:5), lived several thousand years before Abraham. His world became so irredeemably wicked that God destroyed it with a global flood but saved Noah and his family and repopulated the earth through Noah's sons: Shem, Ham, and Japheth (Gen. 6—10).

Christ described the order of events in Noah's days: "For as in the days before the flood, they were eating and drinking, marrying and giving in marriage, until the day that Noah entered the ark, and did not know until the flood came and took them all away" (Mt. 24:38–39).

Then Jesus gave two specific examples of the order at His Second Coming: "Then two men will be in the field: one will be taken and the other left. Two women will be grinding at the mill: one will be taken and the other left" (vv. 40–41).

This is another passage that is often misunderstood. Many people incorrectly use verses 40–41 as examples of the Rapture of the church. Nowhere does the Olivet Discourse deal with the Rapture. It deals with the Second Coming of Jesus Christ. Through these examples, Jesus indicated that, just as some people were taken during the Noahic flood and others were left, some will be taken at His Second Coming and others will not.

Another misinterpretation involves the destiny principle. Some Christians believe this passage teaches God will employ the same destiny principle at Christ's Second Coming that He employed for the Noahic flood, namely, that He will rescue the saved *before* He destroys the unsaved. But this view has problems.

First, in verses 37–39, Christ focused on the pre-flood practices and destiny of the unbelievers of Noah's time, not on a principle of rescuing the saved before destroying the unsaved. Christ emphasized that, instead of preparing for the coming judgment, the unsaved people of Noah's time attended to life's normal activities. Because they did not know when judgment would come, they were ignorant of the deadline for which they needed to be prepared. When the flood came, they were totally unprepared: "The flood came and took them all away" (v. 39). The word *all* indicates not a single unsaved person was left on Earth to enter the period of history after the flood. Such was the order of things when the flood came.

Second, the flood took the people away. God's judgment at Christ's Second Coming will remove unbelievers, as opposed to the Rapture, which will remove believers.

Third, Christ's purpose for His statement "until the day that Noah entered the ark" (v. 38) was not to highlight Noah's destiny but, rather, to identify when the unsaved stopped devoting their attention to the normal activities of life. Hence the word *until*.

Fourth, after focusing on the pre-flood practices and destiny of the unbelievers of Noah's day, Christ said, "so also will the coming of the Son of Man be" (v. 39). He thereby indicated the situation or order of circumstances at His Second Coming will mirror that of the time of the flood. Instead of preparing for judgment, the unsaved at Christ's Second Coming will be focusing on the day-to-day activities of life. Because they will not know when Christ will return (v. 36), they will be utterly unprepared at His coming. Christ will return, and His angels will take all of them away into judgment.

Fifth, Luke 17:26–37 identifies those who will be taken away as unbelievers. Luke recorded the same teaching of Christ that Matthew recorded in Matthew 24:37–41. However, Luke included something Matthew did not: a question Christ's disciples asked Him after He talked about people being "taken" from the bed, mill, and field, while others were "left" at those places at His Second Coming. The disciples asked Christ, "Where, Lord?" (v. 37).

It is important to note the disciples were not asking, "Where will those who will be *left* be?" That question would have been unnecessary since, obviously, those left would remain in the same places they were before the others were taken. Instead, the disciples were asking, "Where will those who will be *taken* be?" They wanted to know where those individuals will end up.

Christ's answer is extremely significant because it identifies *who* will be taken at His Second Coming: "Wherever the body is, there the eagles will be gathered together" (Lk. 17:37). The word translated "eagles" refers to vultures.[2] In this particular verse, the verb translated "will be gathered together" refers to the gathering "of birds of prey around a dead body."[3] So the people taken from the bed, mill, and field will be taken into the realm of death. Death will be part of God's judgment on them, and vultures will eat their dead bodies (cf. Rev. 19:17–18, 21).

By contrast, at the Rapture, the bodies of church saints will be changed into immortal, resurrection-type bodies and transported from the earth to meet Christ in the air (1 Cor. 15:51–53; 1 Th. 4:13–17).

Consequently, Christ's answer indicates it is the unsaved people who will be snatched from their beds, mills, and fields at His Second Coming. They will be taken from Earth in judgment, and not one will be left to enter the next period of history (the 1,000-year Messianic Kingdom) after Christ's return.

On the other hand, all the saved people will be left on Earth in their beds, mills, and fields to enter the Millennium.

Sixth, Jesus taught this same order in His parable of the tares (Mt. 13:37–43). Here, Jesus, the Son of the Man, sows good seeds, who are "the sons of the kingdom," into "the field," which "is the world" (vv. 37–38). "His enemy," the devil, "sowed tares [weeds resembling wheat]," which "are the sons of the wicked one" (vv. 25, 38–39). Jesus interpreted this parable as follows:

> *The harvest is the end of the age, and the reapers are the angels. Therefore as the tares are gathered and burned in the fire, so it will be at the end of this age. The Son of the Man will send out His angels, and they will gather out of His kingdom all things that offend, and those who practice lawlessness, and will cast them into the furnace of fire. There will be wailing and gnashing of teeth. Then the righteous will shine forth as the sun in the kingdom of their Father. He who has ears to hear, let him hear!* (vv. 39–43).

Seventh, Jesus taught this same order again in His parable of the dragnet:

Again, the kingdom of heaven is like a dragnet that was cast into the sea and gathered some of every kind, which, when it was full, they drew to shore; and they sat down and gathered the good into vessels, but threw the bad away. So it will be at the end of the age. The angels will come forth, separate the wicked from among the just, and cast them into the furnace of fire. There will be wailing and gnashing of teeth (vv. 47–50).

Eighth, it should be noted here that the order of circumstances at the Second Coming after the Great Tribulation will be the reverse of the order of events at the Rapture. At the Rapture, Jesus will not return the entire way to Earth. He will stop in the air above the earth, where the church saints "shall be caught up together . . . to meet [Him]" (1 Th. 4:17). They then will return with Him to God the Father's house in heaven. But at Christ's Second Advent, He will come with His church to the earth.

At His last supper with the apostles before He was crucified, Jesus told them He would soon leave to go where they could not yet go (Jn. 13:31–38). That statement disturbed them. To calm them, He declared,

Let not your heart be troubled; you believe in God, believe also in Me. In My Father's house are many mansions; if it were not so, I would have told you. I go to prepare a place for you. And if I go and prepare a place for you, I will come again and receive you to Myself; that where I am, there you may be also (14:1–3).

Thus John 14:1–3 and 1 Thessalonians 4:13–17 reveal that, at the Rapture, Christ will descend to the atmosphere above Earth to remove all church saints and take them to heaven to live with Him in His Father's house. They will remain there until His Second Coming to establish God's Millennial Kingdom after the Great Tribulation. At His Second Coming, they will come with Him to the earth.

His purpose for rapturing the church is so "that where I am, there you may be also" (Jn. 14:3). The apostle Paul, in fact, concluded his comments on the Rapture with a similar statement: "And thus we shall always be with the Lord" (1 Th. 4:17). Both statements teach that once the church saints are raptured to meet Christ in the air, wherever He goes, they will go with Him.

Overall, the context of these passages concerning the Rapture of the church is radically different from the context of Matthew 24:37–44 concerning the days of Noah. Within context, Jesus related the order of events in the days of Noah to the order of things at His Second Coming. Jesus told this parallel to forewarn people on Earth after the Tribulation to respond to the gospel and make certain they are saved before He returns to restore God's theocratic Kingdom. Since no one except God the Father knows the day or hour of the Second Coming (vv. 36, 44), just as the unsaved of Noah's day did not know when God's flood would come, they must not delay.

Jesus' point was this: Just as the flood swept away unbelievers from the earth in Noah's day, so, too, will God's holy angels snatch the unbelievers from the earth when Christ returns. And He will cast them into the furnace of fire, where there will be "wailing and gnashing of teeth" (13:41–42, 49–50).

TWO PARABOLIC ILLUSTRATIONS OF JESUS' WARNING FOR PEOPLE TO BE READY FOR HIS SECOND COMING

In Matthew 24:43–51, Jesus presented two parables to emphasize the urgency of being prepared for His Second Coming after the Tribulation.

THE WATCHFUL HOMEOWNER

The first parable involves a watchful, prepared homeowner (vv. 43–44). Jesus said, "But know this, that if the master of the house had known what hour the thief would come, he would have watched and not allowed his house to be broken into" (v. 43).

A homeowner does not know when a thief will come to rob his house. He could come anytime. So the homeowner must be watchful and prepared to prevent a break-in. Those who make it through the seven-year Tribulation should know that they are in the period immediately preceding Christ's return. So like the homeowner, they must watch and be prepared (by getting saved) for His advent because they do not know precisely when it will occur.

THE FAITHFUL SERVANT AND THE EVIL SERVANT

The second parable contrasts a faithful servant and an evil servant (vv. 45–51). The "faithful and wise servant, whom his master made ruler over his household" (v. 45), is always prepared for his master's appearance. And when the master arrives, he rewards the servant. Likewise, at Christ's Second Coming, Jesus (the Master) will reward those who placed their faith in Him during the seven-year Tribulation. They will receive the privilege of entering into the blessing of God's theocratic, Millennial Kingdom on Earth (cf. 8:10–11; 13:43; 25:34).

By contrast, the unfaithful, evil servant concludes his master is delaying his return home. So he abuses his authority by beating his fellow servants and carousing with drunkards. His master's early return surprises him. He had planned to give his master the false impression that he had properly administered his authority, but his master's early return reveals the servant's evil heart and his extreme abuse of his given authority. As a result, the master "will cut him in two and appoint him his portion with the hypocrites. There shall be weeping and gnashing of teeth" (24:51).

This unfaithful, evil servant represents the people who reject Christ during the Tribulation or shortly thereafter, before His Second Coming. They will not be prepared for Christ's arrival to Earth and, therefore, Christ will judge them severely when He comes. They will not be allowed to enter the theocratic Kingdom that Christ will establish. Instead, they will be removed from the earth and cast into a terrible place of judgment where they will weep and gnash their teeth (13:41–42, 49–50; 22:12–13; 25:30).

CHAPTER 11

Revelation Related to the Future Millennial Kingdom

Matthew 25:1–30

Matthew 24 ends with Jesus warning people to become faithful servants so they can avoid being consigned to a place of torment when He returns to Earth. Through more parables, Matthew 25 continues the warnings to those who will be alive at the end of the Tribulation.

Jesus warns them to make certain they are saved before He comes back to restore God's theocratic Kingdom. It will be urgent they settle that issue in advance because no one except God the Father knows the day or hour of the Second Coming.

As we have seen, when Christ returns, the holy angels will cast all unbelievers into the furnace of fire, where there will be "wailing and gnashing of teeth" (Mt. 13:37–43, 47–50). But the individuals who have placed their faith in Him will go with Jesus directly into God's Kingdom on Earth.

THE PARABLE OF THE 10 VIRGINS

Jesus introduced His first parable in Matthew 25 with the statement, "Then the kingdom of heaven shall be likened to ten virgins who took their lamps and went out to meet the bridegroom" (v. 1). According to New Testament language scholar Johannes Schneider, the Greek word translated "shall be likened" serves "most commonly in Mt. to introduce the parables of the kingdom of God."[1]

Another such scholar, Ethelbert Stauffer, indicated in this parable that Jesus "expresses the meaning and glory of the Messianic period in the images of the wedding and the wedding feast."[2] Thus, he said, the future Kingdom of God is "the great Messianic banquet to which the people of God is invited."[3]

All 10 virgins in the parable have the same purpose: to meet Jesus Christ, the Bridegroom, when He comes to take His bride. It is important to understand here that Jesus' bride will consist of all saved people throughout history, including Old Testament saints. At His Second Coming, He will take them all into His Father's theocratic, Millennial Kingdom on Earth.

In the parable, all 10 virgins intend to follow Jesus and His bride into His Father's Kingdom for the wedding, but not all 10 make it. The word translated "wedding" (v. 10) means "wedding banquet" and is plural. In this context, it refers to "the joys of the Messianic Kingdom."[4] Although the 10 virgins have the same purpose, five are wise and five are foolish. Scholar Georg Bertram said that, in this parable, the word *wisdom* means "preparedness." He explained, "For everything depends on the actual encounter with the Lord, . . . [and it] applies to those who have grasped the eschatological position of man."[5]

The word *foolish* "implies lack of common sense or good judgment."[6] Thus, Bertram wrote, "The parable of the ten virgins has in view approaching judgment. The main admonition is to readiness. For the day and hour when the Lord comes are not known. If the foolish virgins are not ready, it is their own fault. . . . The parable is thus a type of the judgment which . . . men pass on themselves by their own conduct."[7]

The five wise virgins come fully prepared with what is necessary to enter the Kingdom. When the five foolish virgins discover they lack what is necessary, they go looking for it. While the foolish virgins are gone, Jesus comes; and the five wise virgins and others who are ready go with Him into His Father's Millennial Kingdom to partake of its wedding-banquet joys. Once they enter, "the door [is] shut" (v.10). According to language scholar Joachim Jeremias, the shutting of the door "expresses the irrevocable loss of an opportunity" and "carries the sense of judgment."[8]

Later, when the five foolish virgins arrive, they are too late. The door to the Millennial Kingdom is shut permanently. Because they have not fulfilled the requirement necessary to enter before Christ's Second Coming, they are forever doomed to eternal judgment. Despite their begging, "Lord, Lord, open to us!" Jesus answers, "Assuredly, I say to you, I do not know you" (v. 11–12).

Jesus concluded this parable with a warning: "Watch therefore, for you know neither the day nor the hour in which the Son of Man is coming" (v. 13).

THE PARABLE OF THE TALENTS

The parable of the talents in Matthew 25:14–30 involves three servants and somewhat resembles the parable of the faithful and evil servants in 24:45–51. Both address the conduct of servants who are entrusted with the care of their master's possessions in his absence, and both present the consequences of what happens when the masters return and require them to account for their conduct.

> *For it is just like a man about to go on a journey, who called his own slaves and entrusted his possessions to them. To one he gave five talents, to another, two, and to another, one, each according to his own ability; and he went on his journey. Immediately the one who had received the five talents went and traded with them, and gained five more talents. In the same manner the one who had received the two talents gained two more. But he who received the one talent went away, and dug a hole in the ground and hid his master's money* (Mt. 25:14–18, NASB).

The first two Greek words in Matthew 25:14 literally mean "for it is just like" what was said in verse 13: "Watch therefore, for you know neither the day nor the hour in which the Son of Man is coming."[9] In other words, the parable of the talents has the same purpose as the parables in Matthew 24 and 25: to urge people living at the end of the Tribulation to trust Jesus as their Savior before He returns. They must not delay because they will not know the day or hour of His coming, and delay could doom them forever to torment.

The parable of the talents involves a man referred to as "Lord" who has three servants and a sizable amount of wealth consisting of talents (25:20). The Greek word translated "Lord" is *kurios* and refers to "the owner of slaves and property."[10]

The Greek word *doulos* translates as "servant" in the English-language versions of the New Testament. But Greek language scholar Karl Heinrich Rengstorf claims *doulos* "implies obedience to the will of another."[11] He said, "Alongside the will and commission of the *kurios* there is no place for one's own will or initiative.[12] Thus, in essence, the word *doulos* means "slave."[13]

The owner of the three slaves is ready "to go on a journey to a distant country."[14] Due to the distance, he would be gone for a considerable time and could not determine ahead of time how long it would take him to return home. As a result, his three slaves have no idea of the day or hour of his return (v. 14).

Before the master leaves, he entrusts his three slaves with talents. A talent is "a unit of coinage, whose value differed considerably in various times and places, but was always comparatively high."[15] Some Bible commentators say one talent was equal to 15 to 20 years of wages. Whatever its worth, a single talent equaled great wealth. To one slave, the man gives five talents; to another, two talents; and to the third, one talent. He distributes the funds according to each slave's ability and then embarks on his journey. The three slaves are now responsible to care for their master's talents in ways that will benefit him (v. 15).

The Greek text indicates the slave entrusted with five talents went "immediately"[16] to work and gained five more talents for his master (v. 16). Likewise, the slave entrusted with two talents successfully gained two more (v. 17). But the slave entrusted with one talent did not work with it to gain more for the master. Instead, he dug a hole in the ground and buried it. Apparently, he believed he lacked the ability to gain more talents and feared if he tried, he would lose what he had (v. 18).

After a long time, the master finally comes home and settles accounts with his slaves (v. 19). He commends the slave entrusted with five talents because the servant has gained five more. "Well done, good and faithful servant [slave];" the master says. "You were faithful over a few things, I will make you ruler over many things. Enter into the joy of your lord" (vv. 20–21).

The slave entrusted with two talents gives them to his master, plus two more he had gained for him. His master commends him also, saying, "Well done, good and faithful servant [slave]; you have been faithful over a few things, I will make you ruler over many things. Enter into the joy of your lord" (vv. 22–23).

Now comes the slave entrusted with one talent. "Lord," he said, "I knew you to be a hard man, reaping where you have not sown, and gathering where you have not scattered seed. And I was afraid, and went and hid your talent in the ground. Look, there you have what is yours" (vv. 24–25). The word translated "hard" means "harsh, strict, unmerciful."[17] To this slave the master replied, "You wicked [worthless] and lazy servant, you knew that I reap where I have not sown, and gather where I have not scattered seed. So you ought to have deposited my money with the bankers, and at my coming I would have received back my own with interest" (vv. 26–27).

In essence, the master says, "In light of your fear, you should have taken my one talent[18] I entrusted to you to 'experienced money-changers who accept no counterfeit money,'[19] and at least added 'interest'[20] to my talent." The master orders the two productive slaves to take away the worthless slave's talent and give it to the slave who had the 10 talents (v. 28). Then the master explains the basis for his decision: "For to everyone who has, more will be given, and he will have abundance; but from him who does not have, even what he has will be taken away" (v. 29). And with that declaration, the master gives this terrifying command to the two productive slaves: "And cast the unprofitable servant [slave] into the outer darkness. There will be weeping and gnashing of teeth" (v. 30).

The parable of the talents has the same purpose as the earlier parables in Matthew 24 and 25: to emphasize the urgency for people living immediately prior to Christ's Second Coming to trust Christ as their Savior before He returns to restore God's theocratic, Millennial Kingdom. The unsaved people on Earth during that time will be in a precarious situation, one "to be withdrawn or lost at the will of another person."[21] That other person will be Christ.

But this parable also seems to have a second purpose: to indicate that believers who serve Christ well between the time of His ascension to heaven and His Second Coming will be entrusted with reliable ruling positions within His Millennial Kingdom.

Language scholar Werner Foerster wrote, "The goal of the lordship of Jesus in exercise of the Father's sovereignty is thus to make the reconciled and judged world subject to God. In this work, however, man is the crucial point. While the lordship of Jesus is cosmic in scope, its centre is lordship over men."[22] Thus the apostle Paul wrote, "For if we live, we live to the Lord; and if we die, we die to the Lord. Therefore, whether we live or die, we are the Lord's. For to this end Christ died and rose and lived again, that He might be Lord of both the dead and the living" (Rom. 14:8–9).

Rengstorf wrote, "But this authority is Christ. Hence those who work by His commission, represent His cause and must give account only to Him, are rightly called His *douloi*." [23]

CHAPTER 12

The Grand Climax

Matthew 25:31–46

Matthew 25:31–46 presents the great culmination of Christ's Olivet Discourse. The earlier part of the Discourse revealed events leading up to this grand finale that involves Christ's spectacular and unmistakably visible return to Earth, followed by His judgment of the nations.

CHRIST'S GLORIOUS SECOND COMING

Verse 31 introduces the starting point of this grand climax: "When the Son of Man comes in His glory, and all the holy angels with Him, then He will sit on the throne of His glory" (v. 31).

The word translated "when" often approaches the meaning of the Greek word *ean*,[1] which denotes "what is expected to occur, under certain circumstances."[2] Jesus' parables of the watchful, prepared homeowner (24:43–44), the two contrasting servants (vv. 45–51), the 10 virgins (25:1–13), and the talents (25:14–30) all emphasize the fact that the people who will survive the Tribulation will not know the exact time of Christ's Second Coming to Earth. So they should be prepared every hour of every day. The culmination of the Olivet Discourse reveals the awesome implications of their preparation.

When Christ returns, He will come as "the Son of the Man," the last Adam (see chapter 7), "in His glory" (v. 31). The word translated "glory" refers to the outward appearance of "brightness, splendor, radiance."[3] Theologian Gerhard Kittel emphasized that *glory* also means "reputation" and "power" and is "also used strictly in the NT to express the 'divine mode of being.' This is true of all the NT authors."[4] Thus Jesus Christ will return to Earth as God incarnated in human flesh. Jesus Himself indicated as much: "For the Son of Man will come in the glory of His Father with His angels" (16:27). Apparently the brilliant splendor of His deity will radiate through His resurrected human body. Christ's brilliant appearance on the road to Damascus to Saul of Tarsus (later the apostle Paul) may have been a preview of His future, glorious splendor at His Second Coming (Acts 9:1–6; 26:12–18).

Greek language scholar Johannes Schneider claimed the word translated "comes" (Mt. 25:31) refers to "the eschatological coming of the Messiah. . . . Jesus is the promised Messiah who at the end of the days will come in great power and glory" (16:27; 25:31).[5] Schneider pointed out that "the Messianic tribulation" will take place before the eschatological coming of the Messiah to bring "judgment on the one hand and on the other the coming of the Messianic Age of joy in all the glory of its consummation."[6]

When Christ will come from heaven in His glory, it is then that He will sit on the throne of His glory (25:31). During His First Coming, Jesus referred to the future "throne of His glory" (19:28). New Testament language scholar Otto Schmitz claimed the expression *throne of glory* is "used for the sovereign seat of the Son of Man when He is manifested in His Messianic glory to judge and to rule. The reference is to His future rule over the twelve tribes of Israel" (19:28) and "to the judgment exercised on all nations by the Son of Man from this throne" (25:31f).[7]

Scholar Carl Schneider indicated that among the nations in biblical times, "part of the orderly process of a judicial hearing is that the judge should sit in accordance with his dignity."[8] Pilate (Mt. 27:19; Jn. 19:13), Festus (Acts 25:6,17), Herod Agrippa (12:21) and the high priest (23:3) followed this custom.[9] Thus "The Judge [Jesus] of the Last Judgment in the NT is also viewed as sitting, as in other apocalyptic writings (Mt. 19:28; 25:31)."[10]

HOLY ANGEL TASKS

In Matthew 25:31, Jesus revealed that, when He returns in glory to sit on His judgment throne, all the holy angels will come with Him. They will fulfill two major tasks: They will (1) remove all unbelievers from Earth before Christ restores God's theocratic Kingdom and (2) gather the elect of Israel from around the globe. Jesus used parables to demonstrate this teaching.

Matthew 13 records Him teaching parables to great multitudes of people (vv. 1–9). He told His disciples the parables present "the mysteries of the kingdom of heaven" (v. 11). The word translated "mysteries" refers to "the secret thoughts, plans, and dispensations of God which that are hidden from the human reason, as well as from all other comprehension below the divine level, and hence must be revealed to those for whom they are intended."[11] Thus Jesus indicated these parables reveal significant information related to the future theocratic Kingdom.

Two parables in Matthew 13 concern the holy angels' task of removing all the unsaved people from the Earth in conjunction with His Second Coming:

PARABLE OF THE WHEAT AND THE TARES

The first one is the parable of the wheat and the tares (vv. 24–30, 36–43). Here Christ sows the wheat seed, and Satan sows the tares. The wheat represents the saved people, who belong to God's Kingdom, and the tares represent the unsaved. The reapers represent the holy angels who will accompany Christ to Earth at His Second Coming (v. 39).

Before Christ restores God's theocratic Kingdom, He will send out His holy angels to gather all the unsaved people living on Earth. Then these unbelievers will be cast into the furnace of fire, where they will wail and gnash their teeth (vv. 41–42). The saved people will enter the restored theocratic Kingdom of God (v. 43).

PARABLE OF THE DRAGNET

Here Christ used the analogy of a fishing dragnet that was cast into the sea and netted every type of fish. When it was full, the fishermen drew it ashore. They kept the good fish but threw the bad away.

Christ applied this analogy to the future order of events at the end of this present pre-Messianic Age: "The angels will come forth, separate the wicked from among the just, and cast them into the furnace of fire. There will be wailing and gnashing of teeth" (vv. 49–50).

See chapter 9 of this book for a fuller discussion of the gathering of Israel from all over the world (24:29–31).

THE JUDGMENT: THE GATHERING AND SEPARATION OF THE PEOPLE

The Olivet Discourse ends with the judgment of the sheep and the goats. After Christ takes His seat on the judgment throne of His glory as the King of the future theocratic Kingdom, all people from all nations will be gathered before Him. He will separate them into two groups, as a shepherd separates his sheep from the goats (25:32). He will set the "sheep" group on His right, and the "goat" group on His left (v. 33).

Then He will exhort the "sheep": "Come, you blessed of My Father, inherit the kingdom prepared for you from the foundation of the world" (v. 34). Individuals in the sheep group have been saved through faith in Jesus Christ. Just as sheep depend on their shepherd for their destiny, so believers in Jesus Christ depend on Him for theirs. Thus Jesus said, "My sheep hear My voice, and I know them, and they follow Me. And I give them eternal life, and they shall never perish; neither shall anyone snatch them out of My hand. My Father, who has given them to Me, is greater than all; and no one is able to snatch them out of My Father's hand" (Jn. 10:27–29).

According to language scholar Werner Foerster, the word translated "inherit" in Matthew 25:34 "is used to denote the eschatological portion assigned to man."[12]

Two other New Testament passages, Acts 26:18 and Colossians 1:12–14, relate to that future inheritance assigned to believers. When Christ in His resurrected, glorified form appeared to Saul of Tarsus on to the Damascus road, He commissioned Saul to go to the Gentiles "to open their eyes, in order to turn them from darkness to light, and from the power of Satan to God, that they may receive forgiveness of sins and an inheritance among those who are sanctified by faith in Me" (Acts 26:18).

Years later, Saul, now the apostle Paul, exhorted Christians in the city of Colosse to "[give] thanks to the Father who has qualified us to be partakers of the inheritance of the saints in the light. He has delivered us from the power of darkness and conveyed us into the kingdom of the Son of His love, in whom we have redemption through His blood, the forgiveness of sins" (Col. 1:12–14).

Thus when Christ sits on His judgment throne of glory and beckons the people on His right, "Come, you blessed of My Father, inherit the kingdom prepared for you from the foundation of the world" (Mt. 25:34),

He will reveal to them their eschatological inheritance: to dwell in the theocratic Kingdom of God. The word translated "come" is a word of exhortation that urges them to enter this restored theocratic Kingdom.[13]

Language scholar Walter Grundmann pointed out that the word translated "prepared" clearly denotes God's creation and preservation related to heaven and Earth throughout history.[14] The fact that Christ described it as "the kingdom prepared for you from the foundation of the world" indicates it will be a restoration of the theocratic Kingdom of God that God established with Adam at the beginning of Earth's history—the Kingdom that was lost when Satan convinced that first man to disobey God.

THE TWOFOLD DESCRIPTION OF THE "SHEEP"

Christ used two important words to describe the "sheep"—the people on His right: *blessed* and *righteous*. First, He described them as "you blessed of My Father" (v. 34). Language scholar Hermann W. Beyer drew attention to the fact that the basis for God's blessing was established in the Old Testament. That basis consists of trusting God's revealed truth for what embodies proper belief and conduct. Among those blessed were Adam, Noah, Abraham, Moses, and the people of Israel.[15]

King David said,

> *Who may ascend into the hill of the LORD? Or who may stand in His holy place? He who has clean hands and a pure heart, who has not lifted up his soul to an idol, nor sworn deceitfully. He shall receive blessing from the LORD, and righteousness from the God of his salvation* (Ps. 24:3–5).[16]

The prophet Jeremiah recorded the following:

> *Thus says the LORD: "Cursed is the man who trusts in man and makes flesh his strength, whose heart departs from the LORD. For he shall be like a shrub in the desert, and shall not see when good comes, but shall inhabit the parched places in the wilderness, in a salt land which is not inhabited. Blessed is the man who trusts in the LORD, and whose hope is the LORD"* (Jer. 17:5–7).[17]

"The NT," wrote Beyer, "takes over much of the OT concept of blessing."[18] For example, the angel Gabriel called Mary blessed:

Now in the sixth month the angel Gabriel was sent by God to a city of Galilee named Nazareth, to a virgin betrothed to a man whose name was Joseph, of the house of David. The virgin's name was Mary. And having come in, the angel said to her, "Rejoice, highly favored one, the Lord is with you; blessed are you among women!" (Lk. 1:26–28).

Jesus was the ultimate model of blessing people. He picked up, held, and blessed little children (Mk. 10:13–16). He healed many people of illnesses, resurrected individuals who had died, freed people from demonic possession, expanded a small amount of food to feed a huge number of hungry people, calmed a storm that threatened people's lives, forgave those who were guilty of sins, accepted those who were rejected by others, taught the world the beatitudes as a standard guideline for blessedness (Mt. 5:3–12), and voluntarily offered Himself as a sacrifice for the sins of all mankind.

Jesus will explain to the "sheep" on His right why He calls them "blessed of My Father" (25:34). They fed Him when He was hungry, gave Him drink when He was thirsty, brought Him into their homes when He was a stranger, clothed Him when He was naked, visited Him when He was sick, and visited Him when He was in prison (vv. 34–36). In other words, they were more concerned for the welfare of others than for themselves. While focused on helping and blessing others in need, they did not even realize their actions were blessing Christ.

Thus they will answer Him, "Lord, when did we see You hungry and feed You, or thirsty and give You drink? When did we see You a stranger and take You in, or naked and clothe You? Or when did we see You sick, or in prison, and come to You?" (vv. 37–39).

"And the King [Jesus] will answer and say to them, 'Assuredly, I say to you, inasmuch as you did it to one of the least of these My brethren, you did it to Me'" (v. 40).

In addition to "blessed," Christ described these people as "righteous" because they cared for the welfare of the needy. These people will enter the restored theocratic Kingdom of God in conjunction with the Second Coming (v. 37).

THE JUDGMENT OF THE "GOATS"

Not everyone will enter the restored theocratic Kingdom. After Christ tells the blessed, righteous people on His right to enter the restored theocratic Kingdom of God, He will address the "goat" group on His left.

CHRIST'S PRONOUNCEMENT OF JUDGMENT

Jesus will tell this group, "Depart from Me, you cursed, into the ever-lasting fire prepared for the devil and his angels" (v. 41). It is interesting to note that these people will be cursed for the same reason the prophet Jeremiah pronounced cursing in Old Testament times. They will have trusted in themselves, rather than in God: "Thus says the LORD: 'Cursed is the man who trusts in man and makes flesh his strength, whose heart departs from the LORD'" (Jer. 17:5).

New Testament language scholar Seigfried Schulz wrote, "In the last judgment, those who withhold ministering love from their neighbors are directed by the Judge of the world to depart from Him and to go into eternal fire, Mt. 25:41."[19] They will be confined forever in the everlasting fire prepared for the Devil and his angels.

THE REASON FOR JUDGMENT

Christ explained the reason for their judgment: "For I was hungry and you gave Me no food; I was thirsty and you gave Me no drink; I was a stranger and you did not take Me in, naked and you did not clothe Me, sick and in prison and you did not visit Me" (vv. 42–43).

Unbelievers will respond, "Lord, when did we see You hungry or thirsty or a stranger or naked or sick or in prison, and did not minister to You?" (v. 44). Then Christ will say to them, "Assuredly, I say to you, inasmuch as you did not do it to one of the least of these, you did not do it to Me" (v. 45).

The "sheep" (believers) will enter into God's eternal Kingdom, and the "goats" (unbelievers) will be cast into the Lake of Fire: "And these [goats] will go away into everlasting punishment, but the righteous into eternal life" (v. 46).

CONCLUSION

As we have seen, Christ's glorious Second Coming will end Satan's rule, which has plagued the earth since the day Adam defected from God's camp. The Antichrist and his False Prophet will be cast alive into the Lake of Fire burning with brimstone (Rev. 19:11–16, 20). Christ will kill the nations' kings, armies, and other opposition forces; and the birds will eat their flesh (vv. 17–19, 21).

An angel will descend from heaven with the key to the bottomless pit and a great chain. He will bind Satan with that chain and cast him into the bottomless pit where he will be confined and sealed for 1,000 years (20:1–3). Then Christ will restore the theocratic Kingdom of God to planet Earth for those 1,000 years (vv. 4–6).

The Olivet Discourse is an extremely rich portion of Scripture. It is filled with vital information that God wants His people to know concerning His plans for the future. Now that we know, it is my prayer that, as believers who look forward to our Lord's return, we will live worthy of our calling as saints of the Most High God; teach the truths of His Word faithfully; and win as many souls to Christ before it is too late.

ENDNOTES

CHAPTER 1

1   W. Shaw Caldecott, *Herod's Temple* (London: Charles H. Kelly, 1839), 15.

2   John B. Graybill, "Temple," *The New International Dictionary of the Bible*, pictorial ed. (Grand Rapids, MI: Zondervan, 1987), 995.

3   Ibid.

4   Will Durant, *Caesar and Christ* (New York, NY: Simon And Schuster, 1944), 533.

5   Judah David Eisenstein, "Temple in Rabbinical Literature," *The Jewish Encyclopedia* (New York, NY: Funk And Wagnalls, 1907), 12:96.

6   Graybill, 995.

7   William F. Arndt and F. Wilbur Gingrich, eds./trans., "semeion," *A Greek English Lexicon of the New Testament and Other Early Christian Literature* (1952: translation and adaptation of Walter Bauer's *Griechisch-Deutsches Worterbuch zu den Schriften des Neuen Testaments und der ubrigen urchristlichen Literatur*, 4th ed.; (Chicago, IL: University of Chicago Press, 1957), 755. Also, Karl Heinrich Rengstorf, "semeion," *Theological Dictionary of the New Testament* (hereafter cited as *TDNT*), ed. Gerhard Friedrich, trans./ed. Geoffrey W. Bromiley, translated from *Theologisches Worterbuch zum Neuen Testament* (Grand Rapids, MI: Eerdmans, 1971), 7:203, 211, 219, 231–232.

8   Arndt and Gingrich, "semeion," 755.

9   Rengstorf, *TDNT*, "semeion," 232.

10 H. E. Dana and Julius R. Mantey, *A Manual Grammar of the Greek New Testament* (New York, NY: Macmillan, 1927), 147.

11 Arndt and Gingrich, "parousia," 635.

12 Ibid.

13 Gerhard Kittel, "aion," *TDNT*, ed. Gerhard Kittel, ed./trans. Geoffrey W. Bromiley (Grand Rapids, MI: Eerdmans, 1964), 1:206–207.

14 Abraham Cohen, *Everyman's Talmud* (New York, NY: Schocken Books, 1995), 78, 190.

15 Arndt and Gingrich, "blepo," 143.

16 Raphael Patai, *The Messianic Texts* (Detroit, MI: Wayne State

University Press, 1979), 95–96.

[17] Millar Burrows, *More Light on the Dead Sea Scrolls* (Grand Rapids, MI: Baker Book House, 1978), 343–344.

[18] *Sanhedrin* 98b, in *The Babylonian Talmud* (London: Soncino Press, 1935), 665 n "birth pangs of the Messiah."

[19] Patai, 96.

[20] H. J. Fabry, "chebel," *Theological Dictionary of the Old Testament* (hereafter cited as *TDOT*), ed. G. Johannes Botterweck and Helmer Ringgren, eds./trans. David E. Green, translated from *Theologisches Worterbuch zum Alten Testament* (Grand Rapids, MI: Eerdmans, 1980), 4:191.

[21] Arndt and Gingrich, "throeo," 364.

[22] "dei," Ibid., 171.

[23] Walter Grundmann, "dei," *TDNT* (Grand Rapids, MI: Eerdmans, 1964), 2:23.

[24] Fabry, "tsara," *TDOT*, ed. G. Johannes Botterweck, Helmer Ringgren, Heinz-Josef Fabry, trans. Douglas W. Stott (Grand Rapids, MI: Eerdmans, 2003), 12:460.

[25] Gerhard Delling, "arche," *TDNT* (Grand Rapids, MI: Eerdmans, 1964), 1:482.

[26] Georg Bertram, "odin," *TDNT* (Grand Rapids, MI: Eerdmans, 1974), 9:672.

CHAPTER 2

[1] Arndt and Gingrich, "tote," 831.

[2] Ibid., "thlipsis," 362.

[3] Ibid., "miseo," 524.

[4] Ibid., "apostasia," 97.

[5] Heinrich Schlier, "apostasia," *TDNT* (Grand Rapids, MI: Eerdmans, 1964), 1:513.

[6] Arndt and Gingrich, "anomia," 71.

[7] Walter Gutbrod, "anomia," *TDNT* (Grand Rapids, MI: Eerdmans, 1967), 4:1086.

[8] Arndt and Gingrich, "plethuno," 674.

[9] Schlier, 513–514 n 4.

[10] Arndt and Gingrich, "skandalon," 760.

[11] Gustav Stahlin, "skandalon," *TDNT* (Grand Rapids, MI: Eerdmans,

1971), 7:342.

[12] Delling, "plethuno," *TDNT* (Grand Rapids, MI: Eerdmans, 1968), 6:282 n 21.

[13] Arndt and Gingrich, "psucho," 903.

[14] Stahlin, "skandalon," 346.

[15] Ibid.

[16] Arndt and Gingrich, "planao, plane," 671.

[17] Gerhard Friedrich, "prophetes," *TDNT* (Grand Rapids, MI: Eerdmans, 1968), 6:855.

[18] Herbert Braun, "planao," *TDNT* (Grand Rapids, MI: Eerdmans, 1968), 6:247.

[19] Arndt and Gingrich, "hupomeno," 853.

[20] Friedrich Hauck, "hupomeno," *TDNT* (Grand Rapids, MI: Eerdmans, 1967), 4:585.

[21] Arndt and Gingrich, "oikoumene," 564.

[22] Hermann Strathmann, "marturion," *TDNT* (Grand Rapids, MI: Eerdmans, 1967), 4:502–503.

[23] Ibid.

[24] Robert L. Thomas, *Revelation 1–7 Exegetical Commentary* (Chicago, IL: Moody, 1992), 464.

[25] Arndt and Gingrich, "sphragidzo," 804.

[26] Robert L. Thomas, *Revelation 8–22 Exegetical Commentary* (Chicago, IL: Moody, 1995), 204.

[27] Ibid.

[28] Arndt and Gingrich, "heko," 345.

CHAPTER 3

[1] Arndt and Gingrich, "bdelugma," 137.

[2] Ibid., "hagios," 9.

[3] Edward J. Young, *The Prophecy Of Daniel* (Grand Rapids, MI: Eerdmans, 1970), 219.

[4] Arndt and Gingrich, "kairos," 396.

[5] Ibid., "satan," 752.

[6] Victor P. Hamilton, "shup," *Theological Wordbook of the Old Testament* (Chicago, IL: Moody, 1980), 2:912.

[7] Leon Wood, *A Commentary on Daniel* (Grand Rapids, MI: Zondervan, 1973), 323.

8   Ibid.

9   Karl Georg Kuhn, "qadosh," *TDNT* (Grand Rapids, MI: Eerdmans, 1964), 1:89.

10 Ibid., 91.

CHAPTER 4

1   Arndt and Gingrich, "megaley," 498.

2   Ibid., "thlipsis," 362.

3   Delling, "arche," *TDNT* (Grand Rapids, MI: Eerdmans, 1964), 1:481.

4   Arndt and Gingrich, "ou me," 519.

5   Delling, "koloboo," *TDNT* (Grand Rapids, MI: Eerdmans, 1965), 3:823 n 4.

6   Ibid., 823–824.

7   John Calvin, *Commentary on Matthew, Mark, Luke–Volume 2*, ed./ trans. William Pringle (Grand Rapids, MI: Christian Classics Ethereal Library, 1999).

8   Delling, "koloboo," *TDNT* (Grand Rapids, MI: Eerdmans, 1965), 3:823.

9   Arndt and Gingrich, "sarx," 751.

10 D. A. Kidd, "praeter," *Collins Gem Latin Dictionary* (London: Collins Clear-Type Press, 1957), 259.

11 Arndt and Gingrich, "sodzo," 805.

12 Ibid., "elkos," 251.

13 Ibid., "kakos," 398.

14 Ibid., "ponaros," 697.

15 Robert L. Thomas, *Revelation 8–22 Exegetical Commentary*, 275.

16 Ibid., 277.

17 Werner Foerster, "astrape," *TDNT* (Grand Rapids, MI: Eerdmans, 1964), 2:505, n 4.

18 Arndt and Gingrich, "orneon," 585.

19 Ibid., "ptoma," 735.

20 Ibid., "aetos," 19.

CHAPTER 5

1   *Webster's*, 601, s.v. "cosmos."

2   M. Saebo, "yom," *TDOT* ed. G. Johannes Botterweck and Helmer Ringgren, eds./trans. David E. Green (Grand Rapids, MI: Eerdmans,

1990), 6:28–29.

3 Ibid., 30.

4 Ibid.

5 Ibid., 31.

6 R. Mosis, "gadhal," *TDOT* ed. G. Johannes Botterweck and Helmer Ringgren, trans. John T. Willis (Grand Rapids, MI: Eerdmans, 1975), 2:394.

7 B. Kedar-Kopfstein, "meod," *TDOT* ed. G. Johannes Botterweck, Helmer Ringgren, and Heinz-Josef Fabry, trans. Douglas W. Stott (Grand Rapids, MI: Eerdmans, 1997), 8:40.

8 A. Baumann, "kwl," *TDOT* ed. G. Johannes Botterweck, Helmer Ringgren, and Heinz-Josef Fabry, trans. David E. Green (Grand Rapids, MI: Eerdmans, 1995), 7:88.

9 Ibid., 88.

10 J. Schreiner, "pana," *TDOT* ed. G. Johannes Botterweck, Helmer Ringgren, and Heinz-Josef Fabry, trans. David E. Green (Grand Rapids, MI: Eerdmans, 2001), 11:582.

11 Ibid.

12 H. F. Fuhs, "yare," *TDOT* ed. G. Johannes Botterweck and Helmer Ringgren, trans. David E. Green (Grand Rapids, MI: Eerdmans, 1990), 6:293.

13 Ibid., 294.

14 Ibid.

15 Ibid., 295.

16 Ibid., 300.

17 H. P. Muller, "nabi," *TDOT* ed. G. Johannes Botterweck, Helmer Ringgren, and Heinz-Josef Fabry, trans. David E. Green (Grand Rapids, MI: Eerdmans, 1984), 9:150.

CHAPTER 6

1 Grundmann, "dunamai," *TDNT* (Grand Rapids, MI: Eerdmans, 1964), 2:307.

2 Helmer Ringgren, "saba," *TDOT* ed. G. Johannes Botterweck, Helmer Ringgren, and Heinz-Josef Fabry, trans. Douglas W. Stott (Grand Rapids, MI: Eerdmans, 2003), 12:212.

3 Arndt and Gingrich, "satan," 752.

4 Delling, "arxon," *TDNT* (Grand Rapids, MI: Eerdmans, 1964), 1:489.

[5] Werner Foerster, "diabolos," Ibid., 2:80.

[6] Foerster "aer," Ibid., 1:165.

[7] Gerhard von Rad, "diabolos," Ibid., 2:75.

[8] Wilhelm Michaelis, "kosmokrator," *TDNT* (Grand Rapids, MI: Eerdmans, 1965), 3:912.

[9] Gerhard Delling, "arxe," *TDNT* (Grand Rapids, MI: Eerdmans, 1964), 1:483.

[10] Ibid.

[11] Hauck, "koinonos," *TDNT* (Grand Rapids, MI: Eerdmans, 1965), 3:805.

[12] C. E. Van Sickle, *A Political and Cultural History of the Ancient World* (Chicago, IL: Houghton Mifflin Company, 1947), 60.

[13] Grundmann, "ischuo," *TDNT* (Grand Rapids, MI: Eerdmans, 1965), 3:400–401.

[14] Arndt and Gingrich, "methodeia," 500.

[15] *The American College Dictionary*, 1195, s.v. "strategy."

[16] Ibid., 1111, s.v. "shake."

[17] Arndt and Gingrich, "saleuo," 747.

[18] H. E. Dana and Julius R. Mantey, *A Manual Grammar of the Greek New Testament* (New York, NY: Macmillan, 1955), 161.

[19] Mosis, "gadhal," *TDOT* ed. G. Johannes Botterweck and Helmer Ringgren, trans. John T. Willis (Grand Rapids, MI: Eerdmans, 1975), 2:413.

[20] Fuhs, 300.

[21] Grundmann, "dunamai," *TDNT*, (Grand Rapids, MI: Eerdmans, 1964), 2:305.

CHAPTER 7

[1] Rudolf Bultmann, "phaino," *TDNT* (Grand Rapids, MI: Eerdmans, 1974), 9:2.

[2] Ibid.

[3] F. J. Helfmeyer, "oth," *TDOT* ed. G. Johannes Botterweck and Helmer Ringgren, trans. John T. Willis (Grand Rapids, MI: Eerdmans, 1974), 1:183.

[4] Ibid., 171.

[5] Rengstorf, *TDNT*, "semeion," 235.

[6] Arndt and Gingrich, "phula," 876.

7 Rengstorf, "semeion," 237.

8 Stahlin, "kopetos," *TDNT* (Grand Rapids, MI: Eerdmans, 1965), 851.

CHAPTER 8

1 Arndt and Gingrich, "parousia," 635.

2 Ibid.

3 Albrecht Oepke, "parousia," *TDNT* (Grand Rapids, MI: Eerdmans, 1967), 5:870.

4 Wood, 179.

5 Oepke, "nephele," *TDNT* (Grand Rapids, MI: Eerdmans, 1967), 4:905.

6 Arndt and Gingrich, "dunamis," 206.

7 Grundmann, "dunamai," 286.

8 Ibid., 290.

9 Ibid., 291.

10 Ibid., 295.

11 Ibid., 302.

12 Ibid., 305.

13 Arndt and Gingrich, "doxa," 202.

14 Kittel, "doxa," *TDNT* (Grand Rapids, MI: Eerdmans, 1964), 2:247.

15 Arndt and Gingrich, "polus," 694.

16 *Webster's*, 2617, s.v. "theanthropic."

17 Helmet Traub, "ouranos," *TDNT* (Grand Rapids, MI: Eerdmans, 1967), 5:514.

CHAPTER 9

1 Rengstorf, "apostello," *TDNT* (Grand Rapids, MI: Eerdmans, 1964), 1:401.

2 Ibid., 400.

3 Ibid., 399.

4 Francis Brown, S. R. Driver, and Charles A. Briggs, "qadosh," *A Hebrew and English Lexicon of the Old Testament* (Oxford: Clarendon, 1975), 872.

5 G. Quell, "eklegomai," *TDNT* (Grand Rapids, MI: Eerdmans, 1967), 4:163.

6 Ibid., 164.

7 Gottlob Schrenk, "ekloge," *TDNT* (Grand Rapids, MI: Eerdmans, 1967), 4:179.

8 Arndt and Gingrich, "anemos," 64.

9 J. Barton Payne, "riah," *Theological Wordbook of the Old Testament* (Chicago, IL: Moody, 1980), 2:836.

10 Franz Delitzsch, *Biblical Commentary on the Prophecies of Isaiah*, trans. James Martin (Grand Rapids, MI: Eerdmans, 1960), 1:461.

11 Ibid.

12 Friedrich, "salpigx," *TDNT* (Grand Rapids, MI: Eerdmans, 1971), 7:84.

13 Ibid., 80.

14 T. Francis Glasson, *The Second Advent* (London: The Epworth Press, 1963), 199.

15 Ibid., and Delitzsch, 461.

16 Brown, Driver, and Briggs, "nes," 651.

17 Glasson, 198–99.

18 Ibid., 199.

19 Friedrich, "salpigx," quoted from *Apocalypse of Abraham*, 31:1f., *TDOT*, ed. Gerhard Friedrich, trans./ed. Geoffrey W. Bromiley (Grand Rapids, MI: Eerdmans, 1971), 7:84.

20 *The Catholic Encyclopedia* (New York, NY: The Encyclopedia Press, Inc., 1907), 1:604.

CHAPTER 10

1 Hauck, "parabole," *TDNT* (Grand Rapids, MI: Eerdmans, 1967), 5:759.

2 Arndt and Gingrich, "aetos," 19.

3 Ibid., "episunago," 301.

CHAPTER 11

1 Johannes Schneider, "homoiow," *TDNT* (Grand Rapids, MI: Eerdmans, 1967), 5:189.

2 Ethelbert Stauffer, "gameo," *TDNT* (Grand Rapids, MI: Eerdmans, 1964), 1:654.

3 Ibid., 655.

4 Arndt and Gingrich, "gamos," 150.

5 Bertram, "phronimos," *TDNT* (Grand Rapids, MI: Eerdmans, 1974), 9:234.

6 *The American College Dictionary*, 472, s.v. "foolish."

7 Bertram, "moros," *TDNT* (Grand Rapids, MI: Eerdmans, 1967), 4:843.

8 Joachim Jeremias, "thura," *TDNT* (Grand Rapids, MI: Eerdmans, 1965), 3:174.

9 Arndt and Gingrich, "hosper gar," 908.

10 Foerster, "kurios," Ibid., 3:1044.

11 Rengstorf, "doulos," *TDNT* (Grand Rapids, MI: Eerdmans, 1964), 2:274.

12 Ibid., 270.

13 Arndt and Gingrich, "doulos," 204.

14 Ibid., "apodameo," 89.

15 Ibid., "talanton," 811.

16 Ibid., "eutheos," 320.

17 Karl Ludwig and Matin Anton Schmidt, "sklaros," *TDNT*, ed. Gerhard Friedrich, trans./ed. Geoffrey W. Bromiley (Grand Rapids, MI: Eerdmans, 1967), 5:1028.

18 Arndt and Gingrich, "arguros," 104.

19 Ibid., "trapezites," 832.

20 Ibid., "tokos," 829.

21 *The American College Dictionary*, 952, s.v. "precarious."

22 Foerster, "kurios," 1090.

23 Rengstorf, "doulos," 277.

CHAPTER 12

1 Arndt and Gingrich, "hotan," 592.

2 Ibid., "ean," 210.

3 Ibid., "doxa," 202.

4 Kittel, "doxa," 247.

5 Johannes Schneider, "erxomai," *TDNT* (Grand Rapids, MI: Eerdmans, 1964), 2:670.

6 Ibid., 674.

7 Otto Schmitz, "thronos," *TDNT* (Grand Rapids, MI: Eerdmans, 1965), 3:164–165.

8 Carl Schneider, "kathemai," Ibid., 3:442.

9 Ibid.

10 Ibid.

11 Arndt and Gingrich, "musterion," 532.

12 Foerster, "kleros," *TDNT* (Grand Rapids, MI: Eerdmans, 1965), 3:763.

13 Arndt and Gingrich, "deute," 175.

[14] Grundmann, "hetoimadzo," *TDNT* (Grand Rapids, MI: Eerdmans, 1964), 2:704

[15] Hermann W. Beyer, "eulogeo," Ibid., 2:757, 761.

[16] Ibid.

[17] Ibid.

[18] Ibid., 761.

[19] Seigfried Schulz, "poreuomai," *TDNT* (Grand Rapids, MI: Eerdmans, 1968), 6:574.

GENERAL INDEX

SCRIPTURE INDEX